COOKING WITH
HERBS
AND
SPICES

By the same author

Herbs For All Seasons

COOKING WITH HERBS AND SPICES

by
Rosemary Hemphill

with
decorations by
Marianne Yamaguchi

ANGUS & ROBERTSON PUBLISHERS

ANGUS & ROBERTSON PUBLISHERS

Unit 4, Eden Park, 31 Waterloo Road,
North Ryde, NSW, Australia 2113 and
16 Golden Square, London W1R 4BN,
United Kingdom

Fragrance and Flavour *first published by*
Angus & Robertson Publishers, Australia, 1959
Spice and Savour *first published by*
Angus & Robertson Publishers, Australia, 1964
Combined and re-edited edition 1977
Reprinted 1985, 1986

Copyright © Rosemary Hemphill 1977

National Library of Australia
Cataloguing-in-publication data.

Hemphill, Rosemary, 1922-
 Cooking with herbs and spices.

 Bibliography.
 Includes index.
 ISBN 0 207 13549 5.

 1. Cookery (Herbs). 2. Spices.
 I. Yamaguchi, Marianne. II. Title.

641.6'57

Printed in Singapore

CONTENTS

Metric Conversion Tables ix

Introduction 1

HERBS 5

The Herb Garden 7
Growing and Harvesting 13
Growing Herbs Indoors 17
Angelica 20
Balm 22
Basil 25
Bay Leaves 30
Bergamot 33
Borage 36
Chervil 39
Chicory 43
Chives 45
Coriander 48
Dill 50
Fennel 53
Garlic 56
Lavender 59
Marjoram 63
Mint 68
Oregano 74
Parsley 79
Rosemary 83
Roses 88
Sage 92
Savory 97
Scented-leaved Geraniums 101
Tarragon 106
Thyme 111
Herbal Teas 118
Fragrant Gifts 122

SPICES 129

Allspice 131
Cayenne 134
Chili Powder 136
Cinnamon 138
Cloves 142
Curry Powder 146
Ginger 150
Mace and Nutmeg 154
Paprika 157
Pepper 159
Saffron 161
Salt 165
Turmeric 167

AROMATIC SEEDS 171

Aniseed 173
Caraway Seed 176
Cardamom Seed 179
Celery Seed 181
Coriander Seed 183
Cumin Seed 186
Dill Seed 188
Fennel Seed 190
Juniper Berries 193
Mustard Seed 196
Poppy Seed 199
Sesame Seed 202
Vanilla Beans 205

Some Books Consulted 207

Index 208

ILLUSTRATIONS

Between pages:

Basil and Tomato Aspic............ 22-23
Dolmas..................................... 22-23
Seafood Salad 38-39
Fish Special............................. 38-39
Sage Bread........................... 118-119
Noodles and Mushrooms 118-119
Spiced Veal Roll................... 134-135

Between pages:

Bortsch 134-135
French Ice Cream.................... 150-151
Mango Mousse 150-151
Red Cabbage Casserole with Pork
  Sausages, with Mulled Ale ... 166-167
Steak Kebabs with Lemon and
  Mustard Seed Chutney 166-167

ACKNOWLEDGMENTS

The publishers acknowledge with thanks the permission of the copyright owners to reprint the poems "The Sunken Garden", by Walter de la Mare, and "The Clove Orange", by Eleanor Farjeon.

METRIC CONVERSION TABLES

WEIGHTS

Pounds to Kilograms			Ounces to Grams		
	exact measure	accepted measure		exact measure	accepted measure
1	0.45	.5	1	28.35	30
2	0.91	1	2	56.70	60
3	1.36	1.5	3	85.05	90
4	1.81	2	4	113.40	125
5	2.27	2.5	5	141.75	155
6	2.72	3	6	170.10	185
7	3.18	3.5	7	198.45	220
8	3.63	4	8	226.80	250
9	4.08	4.5	9	255.15	280
10	4.54	5	10	283.50	315
			11	311.85	345
			12	340.20	375
			13	368.55	410
			14	396.90	440
			15	425.25	470
			16	453.59	500

LENGTH MEASUREMENTS

inches	mm	cm
1/16	2	
⅛	3	
¼	5	
½	10	1
¾	20	2
1	25	2.5
2	50	5
2½	62	6
3		8
4		10
6		15
7		18
8		20
9		23
10		25
12		30

TEMPERATURES

100 degrees Celsius (boiling point) = 212 degrees
Fahrenheit
0 degrees Celsius (freezing point) = 32 degrees Fahrenheit

Celsius (C.) into Fahrenheit (F.)

deg. C.	deg. F.	deg. C.	deg. F.
120	248	200	392
130	266	210	410
140	284	220	428
150	302	230	446
160	320	240	464
170	338	250	482
180	356	260	500
190	374		

Fahrenheit into Celsius

deg. F.	deg. C.	deg. F.	deg. C.
250	121	400	205
275	135	425	219
300	149	450	233
325	163	475	246
350	177	500	260
375	191		

For oven temperatures degrees Celsius approximately equals half
of degrees Fahrenheit.

	warm		moderate			hot		very hot	
°C	150	160	180	190	200	220	230	250	260
°F	300	325	350	375	400	425	450	475	500

INTRODUCTION

Some herbs, when dried, are known as spices, but these are simply the dried leaves of culinary plants. True spices are aromatic products from various parts of plants usually indigenous to hot countries, where their flavour is at its best. The part required is collected and dried; it may be the buds, bark, berries, fruit, roots, or—as with saffron—the flower stigmas. Nowadays aromatic culinary seeds are generally grouped with spices under that name, and are gathered when ripe from the spent flower-heads of plants.

When dried herbs are used, a much smaller quantity is needed for flavouring than when using herbs picked straight from the garden, for the flavour is more highly concentrated in the dried product. If fresh herbs are called for in a recipe and you do not have them, a fairly general rule to follow is to use one-third of the amount of dried herbs. Usually herbs and spices are meant to complement and bring out the flavour of the dish in which they are being used, not to dominate it, although there are occasions when a greater quantity is called for. I remember eating a friend's delicious apple pie—an old family recipe—with a wonderful pastry dusky with all-spice and cinnamon. A tablespoon of allspice and a dessertspoon of·cinnamon* are sifted with two cups of self-raising flour and a pinch of salt, then stirred with a packed cup of brown sugar, the whole rubbed together

* Level measurements should be used in all the recipes in this book unless otherwise stated.

I

with four ounces of butter and moistened with one well-beaten egg. (I was told to use a little milk if the mixture was not moist enough.) The pastry should be rolled out thinly, divided into two pieces for lining a greased dish and for covering the sugared, lemon-flavoured apples.

Besides their value as flavouring in food, herbs have, of course, traditionally been used in the preparation of medicines. A long time ago man had an affinity with the plant world and a sure, instinctive understanding of it. As Mrs Leyel says in *The Truth About Herbs*, Hippocrates, the "Father of Medicine", was learned in the preparation of herbs, and of a list left by him of four hundred simples (herbs used medicinally, and medicines made from them), half that number are still in general use today. As well as balm, basil, fennel, and thyme, Hippocrates' list included less familiar, slightly sinister-sounding herbs like hemlock, henbane, and mandragora or mandrake, which had the reputation of shrieking when pulled from the ground.

So, whether we grow herbs, eat them, or take them as medicine, they carry us, if we stop to think about them, far back into history. They have been highly important in trade, and wars have been fought over them. In the Middle Ages they were regarded as necessities, not luxuries, for they helped in the preservation of food, as well as being wanted for medicine. They were difficult to obtain, and had to be brought from the Far East first by sea, then by caravan across the desert to be shipped to the great trading ports of Genoa and Venice; then pack animals carried the precious cargo to waiting merchants in northern Europe who finally distributed it. Holland, Spain, France, and Portugal have all struggled at various times to control the spice trade.

When we think of herb gardens established in Europe we may call to mind a rich stew, aromatic with thyme and bay leaves, simmering on the stove in a country kitchen agleam with rows of pots and pans, with geraniums blooming on the window-sill, and a glimpse of a well-stocked herb garden through the shining panes; or, farther back into time, we see a fleeting picture of the garden of some medieval monastery, with its orderly rows of plants cloistered by high walls from the outside world. Beyond that again, herbs and spices take us to hot blue Arabian skies; to hundred-gated Thebes humming with life and trade on the banks of the Nile; to the ancient palace of Knossos on Crete, with its murals of saffron-gatherers; and to the Queen of Sheba herself, visiting King Solomon at Jerusalem: ". . . with a very great company, and camels that bare spices, and gold in abundance, and precious stones."

But while we all enjoy the special magic surrounding the legends of herbs and spices, they are valued above all for their practical uses. These have been affirmed in the writings of many civilizations: Egyptian hieroglyphics, the Old Testament, early Greek and Roman documents, Saxon and medieval manuscripts, and the great English herbals of William Turner, John Gerard, and John Parkinson. When reading any history of herbs and spices one is struck by the common sense with which they have been used. Aniseed, for instance, has digestive qualities, and so we read of the Romans finishing their sumptuous feasts with anise cakes. Dill seed has the same attribute, and is often included in old recipes for cooking cabbage, to make this vegetable more digestible. And this combination of romance and practicality continues to the present day. Many national or regional dishes rely on a particular herb or spice for their special character: paprika is the spice which imparts to Hungarian goulash its distinctive flavour and colour; chili powder gives Chile con Carne its fire; Spaghetti Bolognese is not complete without

3

oregano; while saffron in Bouillabaisse is traditional.

It is interesting that some herbs differing widely in appearance and flavour belong to the same family. For instance, mint, thyme, basil, and rosemary are all members of the large family Labiatae, recognized by their square stems and two-lipped flowers. And tarragon, one of the most popular culinary herbs, belongs to a family (Compositae) which numbers among its members such plants as chrysanthemums, lettuce, the common daisy, and asters: these plants have composite flower-heads made up of tightly clustered florets, hence the botanical name given to the family.

THE HERB GARDEN

I know a bank whereon the wild thyme blows,
Where oxlips and the nodding violet grows
Quite over-canopied with luscious woodbine,
With sweet musk-roses, and with eglantine . . .
A Midsummer Night's Dream. OBERON, ACT II, SCENE I.

IT IS IN THE PLANNING AND PLANTING OF GARDENS THAT many people express their sense of the beautiful and find contentment. To some it may be the simple joy of stepping on to a peppermint-scented carpet of penny-royal in the early morning; to others the pleasure of seeing the jewelled flowers of a favourite tea-tree glistening through the mistiness of a spider's web.

Originally man depended on plants for food and medicine, and many of the ornamental flowers, shrubs and trees that are part of the garden landscape today, were once valued for their healing properties as well as for their beauty. All through history there have been stories of gardens—from the splendour of the Hanging Gardens of Babylon, one of the seven wonders of the ancient world, to the monastic "physic gardens" of medieval days, where monks grew herbs and concocted them into healing potions and salves for the sick.

There is an interesting biblical tale, nearly 2000 years old, told in *The Bible as History*, of the herbal gardens of the village of Mataria, near Cairo—the Queen of Sheba is said to have taken seeds of balsam as a present to King Solomon, and scented bushes from the seeds grew in Jericho. Many years later Cleopatra took cuttings of these valuable plants to Mataria. Later still, during their flight into Egypt, Joseph, Mary, and Jesus took refuge in these fragrant balsam gardens of Mataria.

It is said that in ancient Egypt the homes of the nobles on the river Nile had cool gardens within the courtyards, the floors of which were exquisitely tiled by craftsmen to show flowers, grasses and birds, which were, centuries later, revealed to excavators. The love of gardens has stayed inherent in us and today we have landscape windows, and doors opening on to vine-covered terraces, bringing "the outdoors in" for a restful and harmonious atmosphere.

The garden where scented plants grow has a strong attraction, particularly for the winged creatures that bring life to any garden. Bees, especially, love bergamot or bee-balm, and borage too, which is, incidentally, often grown as a crop for bees; buddleia, with its trusses of soft, purple flower-heads similar to lilac blossom, brings flocks of butterflies, and if there are a few berry trees and a trough of water in the garden, birds will be found there chattering and splashing and appreciating it all.

My grandfather always thought of the birds in his garden in Kent. There were bird-baths, and bird-tables for crumbs and seed, carefully placed over the four acres of his garden, and in winter there were lumps of suet and halved coconuts hanging from the trees to nourish the birds when times were lean during the cold weather.

This was the garden, "New Farm", mentioned in the *Memoirs of Lady Hester Stanhope*, William Pitt's niece, to which she used to ride over to admire the yew trees. The trees are no longer there, the garden now being only a memory, with rows of houses standing in its place.

For the sake of Shakespeare's lines sung by Oberon, it

would be fitting to add to a scented garden the age-old enchantment of honey-laden thyme; oxlips (*Primula elatior*) one of the primrose family; "the nodding violet" with its fresh, sweet scent; "luscious woodbine", which is honeysuckle; eglantine, the sweet briar rose and the musk rose (*Rosa moschata*). Eleanour Sinclair Rohde, the English authority and writer on herbs, says: "The true musk rose has single white blooms borne in large trusses. . . . *R. moschata* is also a parent, or rather, grand-parent, of such famous roses as Cloth of Gold."

A scented garden is not complete without a variety of herbs, and they are very interesting to grow. Each plant has its own characteristic flavour and scent, which may be utilized in cooking, in making fragrant and beneficial "tisanes" (nourishing decoctions) or gathering and drying for pot-pourri or sweet sachets. Every herb has its own legend too, and it is almost worth growing them for this alone.

Although herbs may grow among all the other plants in the garden, it is more satisfactory to have them to-gether—you are not then wondering if the thyme is hid-ing under the jasmine, or if you will have to disturb the columbines to find the chives! When the herbs are grow-ing together it is an easy matter to survey them at a glance and decide which ones you would like to pick and put in sandwiches, or in a rice salad, or use in other ways.

Herb sandwiches have a fresh and pleasing flavour—everyone likes them. Spread slices of brown bread—brown seems to go best with herbs—with butter and a little cream cheese or marmite, fill with chopped herbs and cut off the crusts. Almost any herbs will do, although it is wise to use a little discretion; for instance, marjoram and basil are pungent and go well with chives or parsley. Pennyroyal, which has a strong flavour of peppermint, is

9

best mixed with parsley and a leaf of two of eau-de-Cologne mint; mustard and cress are old favourites, and on very hot days spearmint sandwiches are refreshing.

In the early morning and in the evening, when there are shadows and the light is soft, I am reminded of Walter de la Mare's poem, "The Sunken Garden",

Speak not ——— whisper not;
Here bloweth thyme and bergamot;
Softly on the evening hour,
Secret herbs their spices shower.
Dark-spiked rosemary and myrrh,
Lean-stalked, purple lavender;
Hides within her bosom, too,
All her sorrows, bitter rue.

Breathe not ——— trespass not;
Of this green and darkling spot,
Latticed from the moon's beams,
Perchance a distant dreamer dreams;
Perchance upon its darkening air,
The unseen ghosts of children fare,
Faintly swinging, sway and sweep,
Like lovely sea-flowers in the deep;
While, unmoved, to watch and ward,
Amid its gloomed and daisied sward,
Stands with bowed and dewy head
That one little leaden Lad.

It is possible for everyone to grow herbs, whether their garden is large or small, or even if they have no garden. People living in flats may grow many herbs sucessfully in suitable containers; details of how this may be achieved are given in the chapter Growing Herbs Indoors.

Nearly all herbs prefer light, well-drained soil and plenty of sunlight so that they may produce their essential oils. The few that prefer shade and a moist position, such as angelica, bergamot and chervil may be planted in the shadiest corner, perhaps under a lemon-scented verbena tree, and given the water they require.

A sunny pathway planting of herbs within easy reach of the kitchen has endless possibilities, and a sundial set at a pleasing angle gives interest. Sundials for the southern hemisphere are available. A base may be made of stones cemented together, or an old tree stump of the right size is quite effective.

A wheel-garden or a ladder-garden makes compact plantings. For a wheel-garden, lay an old cartwheel on prepared ground, and plant the herbs between the spokes with either a sundial or a tall, bushy perennial, such as rosemary, wormwood, sage or lavender in the middle. Graduate the size of the other herbs as they radiate from the centre, with the low border plants, chives, parsley, pennyroyal and thyme for instance, at the edges. For a ladder-garden, lay the ladder along the ground, and plant herbs between the rungs.

For a larger garden, a corner might be found for a properly enclosed herb garden laid out with geometrical beds. These gardens may vary in size and shape from perhaps a square garden 10 feet by 10 feet to a rectangular garden 18 feet by 25 feet or larger. It is a matter of taste and room. There are various ways of enclosing a garden like this; for a formal effect a low hedge of clipped dwarf box (*Buxus sempervirens*) is traditional, neat and attractive. A scented hedge of either French lavender, hyssop, "lad's love" (*Artemisia abrotanum*), winter savory or rosemary is equally as good. The garden may also be enclosed with crossed saplings for climbing roses to grow over, or a low picket fence, painted white. Brick or stone is used, too, and even though this takes more time to construct it is very attractive when completed.

For those who may wish to attempt a garden of this kind, the following description of a typical one will serve as a guide. An area 25 feet by 18 feet was pegged out and surrounded with a wall, 3 feet high, of "ballast" stone. The stones were cemented together, not too neatly, so as to give them a rough, weathered look. The wall was made double, with a space in the middle about 12 inches wide to contain soil for plants to grow in. Holes were left in the cement for drainage.

In the middle of the garden there is a sundial, with simple geometrical beds of herbs and stone paths radiating from it. There is also a stone seat, with English lavender growing on either side of it. The same sweet-smelling plant borders the little pathway leading from the herb garden into the rose garden.

With a garden of this type, shrubs and plants of varying heights may be grown from the top of the wall very effectively. Sturdy French lavender, prostrate rosemary, creeping thymes, wormwood, lavender-cotton and the old, scented wallflower are just a few that are suitable.

Whatever the size of your herb patch, it will give you joy, and if you have not grown herbs before, there is a new adventure in fragrance and flavour waiting for you.

GROWING AND HARVESTING

WHEN PLANNING TO GROW HERBS, HAVE THE POSITION AND ground ready in time for planting in spring. A sunny aspect and light soil is a good all-round rule for growing herbs. A few such as chervil, bergamot and angelica prefer semi-shade, and this may be arranged by choosing the most protected position for them.

Sow the seeds in seed boxes after the frosts are over, and, when big enough to handle, plant the seedlings out. If well cared for they will grow rapidly and be ready to start using within a few weeks. Water them in dry weather and keep them weeded and cultivated.

Herbs respond to constant picking: chives become sturdier and send out fresh, tender leaves more quickly; parsley and chervil leaves should be picked from the outside always, allowing the new leaves to grow from the middle; basil must have the tops continually picked out to make a sturdy bush and to prevent it from flowering too soon.

The low-growing herbs best suited for edging are pennyroyal, chives, fragrant thyme, chervil, variegated balm and hyssop. Herbs of medium height are spicy tarragon, coriander, sweet basil, oregano, winter savory, mint, marjoram, lemon balm and chamomile. The taller herbs to use for background planting or to feature as a central point are angelica, lovage, basil, dill, fennel, sage, lavender, rosemary, rue, anchusa and chicory. Bergamot must be cherished in a sheltered, rather moist position.

Mint and tarragon must have room to spread, so it is wise to remember this when planting. Borage is lovely if left to itself and allowed to grow in a misty blue drift in a corner on its own.

The perfumed herbs should be grown for making into scented gifts, or to pick for fragrant posies or "tussie-mussies" as they were once called. Many of them are used to impart their aroma to certain food. There are the lavenders—English (*Lavandula vera*) and French (*L. dentata* and *L. stoechas*), to name but three varieties. Rosemary is used sparingly in cooking veal and pork dishes, but it is more often grown for its sweet scent and meaning of friendship and remembrance. Rue is the "herb of grace" and should be nearby, for "where there's rosemary there's rue". A small amount of the chopped leaves are often used in vegetable cocktails.

Scented-leaved geraniums are also used in flavouring some foods, but are better known for the fragrance of their leaves. Lemon-scented verbena grows into a graceful tree with deliciously perfumed leaves which retain their lemon scent long after they have been dried and are brittle with age; a few fresh leaves impart a delicate flavour when baking milk puddings. Heliotrope or "cherry pie" is a soft cloud of mauve when in full bloom and is one of the most fragrant herbs; grow it in a sheltered sunny position.

Wallflowers, the old yellow and tawny ones, contain in the flowers the distilled essence of all the mellow summer scents, warm walls, new-mown hay and the sweetness of all flowers; this plant was once a healing herb. Added to the few which have been mentioned are other well-known plants which were once valuable herbs —roses, violets, jasmine, primroses, clove-pinks, hollyhocks, foxglove and honeysuckle, all of which would be in keeping in a herb garden.

Have you ever thought of having a herb lawn, or a pathway made entirely of herbs? Thyme, pennyroyal and chamomile are all suitable for this. The hardy *Thymus serpyllum*, if given a chance to establish itself, makes a fragrant carpet. It can not bear much traffic, so it would have to be grown in a special corner of its own. Thyme, grown over a mound of earth, makes a soft and scented seat; plant established roots, lift apart in the early spring and keep weed-free and well-watered.

Pennyroyal spreads very quickly, is extremely hardy, and discourages weeds once it has formed a thick mat. The fresh peppermint scent is released when trodden on, and it would be a pity to mow it in the spring when its small spires of lavender-coloured flowers are in bloom making a "fairy mead". Plant roots two to three feet apart in the spring and autumn.

English chamomile (*Anthemis nobilis*) is the only one of the three which needs mowing. E. S. Rohde says: "I wonder how many of the people who attend the royal garden parties at Buckingham Palace realize that big stretches of one of the lawns are planted with camomile?" It makes an excellent lawn and is particularly hardy in hot, dry weather, remaining green and fresh-looking. It may be walked on as much as an ordinary grass lawn. Put in the plants 4 inches apart in spring or autumn, roll it and weed and water it. Paths of these carpeting herbs may replace stone or brick paths in the herb garden.

As the season advances and the herbs approach maturity it is time to decide those to dry for winter use. Although leaves of marjoram, thyme and oregano are always available, they are even more pungent when dried, and now is the time, while the atmosphere is dry, to do it. Herbs should be harvested just before the buds open into full flower for the greatest flavour and abundance of oils.

Gather them in dry weather, after the dew has left them and before the hot sun has drawn out the natural oils, hang them up to dry in bundles in an airy passageway, or lay them on paper in a dark cupboard. Oven-drying is not good unless wet weather makes it necessary, as much of the flavour is lost in this way. The drying time varies from about twelve days to three weeks. When dry, strip the leaves from the stalks on to clean paper and pour them into clean, dry, airtight jars which have been clearly labelled. Keep the herbs separate so that blending becomes a personal choice. It is interesting to experiment with flavours.

With the coming of autumn in the herb garden, the flowers which have been left to bear next season's crop of herbs must be gathered when the seeds are ripe. Put the seeds away in labelled airtight envelopes or little jars. Cut out dead stalks in the garden and trim the plants.

When winter comes sweet basil will be missed, but instead there are fresh marjoram leaves which are very aromatic and pungent and seem to suit the season; winter vegetables after all have stronger flavours.

By mid-winter the herb garden will be lying dormant, waiting for spring, and as many of the herbs are perennials, their second year will be worth seeing. It is a good idea at this time to give the ground a light top-dressing of well-decayed poultry humus.

When spring comes again and the garden is established, it is time to think of the other aspects connected with herb gardening. The sweet-smelling herbs, flowers and fruit needed for making pot-pourri, lavender bags, sachets, pomander oranges, herb pillows, scented coat-hangers and perfumed rubbing lotions are ready. These make delightful and unusual gifts at Christmas.

Kind thoughts surround sweet smelling things, and it is pleasant to carry on this old tradition.

GROWING HERBS INDOORS

PEOPLE WHO LIVE IN FLATS AND WOULD LIKE TO GROW HERBS
may do so successfully if a few simple rules are followed.
First of all the right soil mixture is important, and it
should consist of sand, leaf-mould and soil in equal parts.
Nurseries sometimes sell this mixture in polythene bags.
Secondly, herbs love sunlight so at some stage during
the day it is desirable for them to bask in it, particularly
by an open window. The third point to remember is to
keep them watered—once a day should be sufficient.
About once a fortnight add a little liquid fertilizer, which
is obtainable at most nurseries, to the watering can.

When planting, cover the hole in the container with
a few pieces of broken crock or some stones, and then
fill with soil. Put in the seedlings, firming them well with
the hands, and water well.

Nearly all herbs will grow in containers, the taller-
growing varieties such as Florence fennel, borage and
sage becoming satisfactorily dwarfed with the confined
root-space. The herbs of low and medium growth, sweet
basil, chervil, chives, marjoram, parsley, and thyme are
all excellent for this purpose. Herbs with rampant root
systems, for instance balm, winter savory, the mints,
origano, pennyroyal and tarragon should be put severely
on their own, or they will choke out the others. Lavender,
rosemary, and the scented-leaved geraniums will not
attain the height they would reach if growing in the
garden, but if re-potted every year with new soil, and
when necessary given a larger container, they will give

pleasure for a very long time. Angelica, chicory and lovage grow too high to be considered.

There are various containers on the market suitable for growing herbs in, and, starting from the kitchen, here are a few suggestions: pots of terra-cotta or china grouped on kitchen window ledges are excellent and may be moved about for convenience; let the mint run riot in a squat six-inch azalea pot; a trough of tin, cement or terra-cotta on the window-sill with several herbs grouped together, is convenient, a good combination being marjoram, chives and parsley, although this is really a matter of personal choice. A graceful, black wrought-iron stand on inch-high legs filled with herbs in china pots, or a trough fitted snugly into it, may be used either on a kitchen window-sill or as a centrepiece on the dining-room table. It is delightful to look at and amusing to snip off the leaves to flavour a French salad to be mixed at the table.

As wrought iron is light and airy it is particularly suitable for flats, whether large or small, blending with any type of furniture and all styles of decoration.

For balconies, roof gardens, back doors or where space is otherwise restricted, a large "strawberry pot" with from six to nine pockets is a good idea. The procedure for filling this container is to prepare the soil and put in the plants as the pot is filled with earth, leaving the most decorative herb until last for the top. The soil may be bought ready mixed, or it may be prepared by mixing equal quantities of sand, leaf-mould and soil. With this light soil, water reaches every herb, right down to the bottom. Experiments have shown that a heavier soil combination is a failure. The sand is necessary to prevent the soil from clogging, and the leaf-mould is important for airiness and fertilizing, and as mentioned earlier, this mixture is excellent for other types of containers also.

Let imagination help you in deciding the containers and stands to use. Secondhand or antique shops are a treasure-trove to discerning eyes. With a little paint or polish the most unlikely article may turn out to be an original and striking holder.

ANGELICA

As its name suggests, the perennial herb angelica (*Angelica archangelica*), has heavenly associations in ancient folklore. In her book *Herbs and Herb Gardening* E. S. Rohde says traditionally an angel revealed its qualities in a dream during a time of plague, and a piece of the root held in the mouth was commended to drive away the "pestilentiall aire".

It was very highly regarded in the old herb gardens, every part of the plant having some particular use. Today, oil distilled from the seeds and roots is used in flavouring liqueurs and wines and the leaves are used in making beneficial tisanes, and for flavouring stewed fruit. Candied angelica is well known, the stalk and leaf stems being used for this.

Angelica grows up to six feet in height, and unlike most herbs prefers a moist, rich soil and shade. The seed will not germinate unless it is very fresh.

CANDIED ANGELICA

It is well worth while candying your own angelica; it is not much trouble, but takes a little time. If you plan ahead and quick results are not expected, then you are half way to having it done.

Select young stems and stalks of angelica. Cut into 4 or 5 inch lengths and place in a glass or crockery vessel, pour over them a boiling solution of 1 pint water and ¼ lb. salt. Cover and leave for 24 hours. Lift out, drain on a wire drainer, peel and wash in cold water.

Make a syrup of 1½ lb. sugar and 1½ pints water, and boil

for ten minutes. Place the angelica in the boiling syrup for 20 minutes; lift out and drain for 4 days on a wire drainer.

Reboil again for 20 minutes in the same syrup. Allow to cool in the syrup, lift out and drain for three or four days. Strew well with sugar and store in airtight jars.

Trifles and cakes are decorated with candied angelica cut into leaves, stems and fancy shapes, and that delightful Italian sweet cassata has angelica in it.

STEWED RHUBARB AND ANGELICA LEAVES

1 *bunch rhubarb*
1 *cup water*
½ *cup sugar*

4 *young angelica leaves*
2 *thin curls of lemon peel*

Cut up rhubarb and put in saucepan with water, sugar, lemon peel and angelica leaves. Bring to boil and simmer until tender.
Serve chilled with whipped cream or yoghurt.

GLAZED PEARS

4 *large pears thoroughly dry*
1 *cup passion-fruit pulp*
1 *cup water*
½ *cup sugar*

Angelica
1 *teaspoon cinnamon or*
   4 *coriander seeds*
A little butter

Wash and core pears from the stalk end. In each hollow put a knob of butter, a little sugar and cinnamon, or 1 coriander seed. Place in a saucepan and pour over them a syrup made from the sugar and water boiled together for 10 minutes. Cover and simmer slowly until just tender, ladling the syrup over continually. Add the passion-fruit pulp.

Lift the pears out carefully and put on a dish. Pour the passion-fruit and syrup over the pears. Decorate each pear with a stalk of angelica. Chill, and serve with heavy cream.

Instructions for making angelica tea are given in the chapter Herbal Teas.

BALM

Balm (*Melissa officinalis*) is an easy perennial plant to grow. Like the mint family it prefers part shade and a moist position, and in the autumn it should be cut down to the ground. It has quite a rampant root system, but is easy to keep in check.

In spring the young lemon-scented leaves are fresh and attractive, and it grows rapidly into a thick and bushy plant about two-and-a-half feet high. In summer the series of small, white flowers carried on long stems are a great attraction to bees.

Balm was indispensable in the old herb garden. Refreshing teas and healing ointments were made from the leaves, and bee hives were often rubbed with it. The leaves are a valuable ingredient in pot-pourri too, the rather piercing lemon scent complementing some of the sweeter flower scents. A pot-pourri should be like well-cooked food that has many ingredients in its composition, the whole being a pleasing blend, but no one flavour or aroma being too predominant.

Balm, or lemon balm as it is sometimes called, dries well and retains its scent. A few dried leaves put in the teapot with your usual Indian tea makes an invigorating drink for fatigue, and in hot weather is refreshing.

Variegated balm (*M. officinalis variegata*) is grown more for its appearance than for practical purposes, although a leaf floated on top of an iced drink looks attractive. It is a perennial, of spreading habit, growing

Basil and Tomato Aspic
(p. 28).

no more than twelve inches high, and is most effective with its green and pale-gold foliage for rockeries, borders, and in flower arrangements too. It is very aromatic, the whole plant smelling of lemons. It must be watered in dry weather, and protected from too much frost.

The following recipes are for lemon balm, as it is hardier, but a few leaves of the variegated type are suitable for garnishing.

BALM AND MARSHMALLOW CUSTARD

1 pint milk
2 eggs
1½ tablespoons sugar
6 marshmallows
1 vanilla bean

1 tablespoon fresh balm leaves, or 1 dessertspoon dried and crumbled balm leaves

Put the marshmallows in the bottom of a well-buttered fireproof dish. Whisk the eggs and sugar together, add milk, beat well and pour over the marshmallows. Put in the vanilla bean, and sprinkle the balm leaves on top. Place the dish in a shallow pan of cold water and bake slowly in a medium oven until set.

Serve chilled with cream—it seems to go particularly well with slices of fresh sugared pineapple.

BALM AND ORANGE FROSTED
(A refreshing summer drink.)

2 cups orange juice
1 cup lemon juice
1 pint water
2 bottles ginger ale

1 bunch balm leaves
½ cup sugar
Ice cubes

Mix juices, balm leaves, sugar and water and chill overnight. Strain, add ginger ale just before serving and pour into glasses over cubes of ice. Float a balm leaf on the top of each drink.

Dolmas (p.27).

The following salad is excellent with roast duck. It may also be served with turkey or ham.

BALM DRESSING FOR ORANGE SALAD

Peel 4 large oranges, cut in sections and lay in a dish with thinly sliced green peppers. Make a French dressing (1 tablespoon herb vinegar to 3 tablespoons oil) and stir in 1 tablespoon of finely chopped balm. Pour over the oranges and allow to marinade for a few hours before serving.

BASIL

Once having used basil in cooking you will think of the two as synonymous, although the story of "Isabella and the Pot of Basil", immortalized in John Keats's poem is probably more often associated with its name. Do not let that rather grisly tale turn you aside from this truly wonderful herb, for the whole plant has a unique mouth-watering aroma which is released at the merest touch and makes you want to pick it at once and use it in all sorts of ways.

A frost-tender annual plant with a delicate, spicy flavour, basil originally came from India, where as *tulasi* it was used in many religious and superstitious rites. Other countries adopted it centuries ago, and it figures prominently in Greek, Italian, and French cooking.

The two varieties that are the most useful and easy to grow are sweet basil (*Ocimum basilicum*) and bush basil (*O. minimum*). They are both annuals, bush basil growing only to a height of six inches or so. If sown in a warm, sunny position in light, rich soil after the frosts, sweet basil will grow to a height of two feet until frosty weather again.

Once the plant is established, keep nipping off the tops, a process that will make it branch out and spread into a sturdy bush. The nipped tops should not be thrown away but used. Once you have let the plant flower, which it tries to do very early and is one of the reasons for nipping, it can be cut right down, and the branches hung up to dry for winter use.

Although this herb is more pungent when fresh, it retains its flavour well when dried and is always useful when cooking tomatoes. When thoroughly dry, rub the leaves and flowers off the stalks onto paper and pour into clean, dry airtight jars.

Basil is known best for its affiliation with tomatoes. It is delicious when chopped and sprinkled on circles of ice-cold, red tomatoes, on baked tomatoes, in tomato puree and in tomato juice. There are endless ways of using it with tomatoes. It is not, however, limited for using with this vegetable. It combines well with eggs, in potato salad, mixes well in a cold rice salad, and it imparts its flavour when added to soups and stews.

Cold rice salad, laced generously with chopped green herbs with basil predominating, is excellent. Boil the rice in the usual way and empty it into a colander, run cold water over it to separate the grains, leave it to drain and cool, then turn it into a bowl. There are endless varieties of ingredients to put with it from prawns, olives, nuts, grated onion and diced celery to chopped ham or bacon, asparagus tips, tomatoes and cucumber cut into chunks and slivers of cheese. Pick sprays of fresh basil from the garden, remove the leaves and chop them very finely and put them into the bowl before adding the dressing—make a French dressing in the usual way by mixing together in a cup 1 tablespoon of white vinegar or herb vinegar, and 3 tablespoons of olive or peanut oil, salt, pepper and a dash of sugar—just before serving pour this dressing onto the rice salad and toss well.

Basil makes a savoury vinegar. It is simply made by packing the fresh leaves into a jar and pouring 1 pint of white vinegar over them. Cover tightly and allow to infuse on a sunny shelf for two weeks. Strain and use in French dressing.

FRENCH DRESSING

1 *tablespoon white or herb vinegar*
3 *tablespoons olive oil, or peanut oil*
Salt, pepper and a pinch of sugar

Mix these ingredients together in a small basin or cup, and toss a salad with it immediately before serving.

BAKED TOMATOES AND BASIL

1 *lb. tomatoes*	*Breadcrumbs*
2 *onions*	*Butter, sugar, salt and*
1 *tablespoon chopped basil*	*pepper*

Slice the tomatoes and onions. Put a layer of tomatoes in the bottom of a buttered pie dish, then a dessertspoon of basil and a layer of onions. Season with salt and pepper, a sprinkling of sugar and dot lightly with butter. Repeat this until the dish is full then top quite thickly with bread-crumbs and pieces of butter. Bake in a moderate oven for 20 minutes. The tempting aroma that greets you when this is taken from the oven is delicious. Serve it hot with roast beef or lamb.

LAMB'S FRY WITH BASIL

As basil and lamb's fry go well together, the following recipe is a particularly good one.

1 *lamb's fry*	2 *tablespoons chopped basil*
Flour seasoned with salt	½ *lb. bacon*
and pepper	*Butter or margarine*

Fry the bacon and put on a dish in a warm place. Melt the shortening, and gently cook the fry which has been cut up and rolled in the flour. At the last add the basil and 1 cup of stock and a little wine if liked. Arrange the fry with the bacon, and pour the gravy from the pan over. Serve hot.

DOLMAS

An unusual way of serving liver with a green vegetable, both aromatically spiced with basil, is shown in this recipe for stuffed leaves of cabbage, spinach, or, if you have a grape-vine, vine leaves.

Cabbage or spinach	*1 onion, chopped*
1 lb. lamb's fry	*1 cup cooked rice*
2 oz. butter or margarine	*2 teaspoons basil*
2 cloves of garlic, finely	*Several rashers of fat bacon*
chopped	*2 tablespoons red or white*
1 red or green capsicum,	*wine, stock, or water*
chopped	*Salt and pepper*

Allow 3 or 4 cabbage, spinach, or vine leaves for each person. Wash the leaves selected for stuffing, cut out any hard stalk, blanch in boiling water for a few minutes, and drain. Soak the lamb's fry in salted water, remove the skin, and chop the meat into small pieces. Melt the butter in a saucepan then soften the onion, garlic, and capsicum in it. Add the meat and allow it to cook gently, turning frequently. Stir in the rice and basil and season with salt and pepper.

Spread out the blanched leaves, put mounds of meat and rice mixture on each one, and roll up into parcels. Place in layers in a casserole with pieces of bacon between the layers and on top. Pour in the liquid and put the casserole lid on. Bake in a slow oven (250°F.) for 1½ to 2 hours. If during the cooking it becomes a little dry, add more liquid.

BASIL AND TOMATO ASPIC

A smooth-textured and delicately flavoured aspic. Prepare it a day or so beforehand and keep it chilled in the refrigerator, unmoulding just before serving. Accompany with thin slices of ham, a tossed green salad, and hot rolls.

2 pints tomato juice	*1 dessertspoon basil*
1 cup mayonnaise	*2 tablespoons lemon juice*
3 envelopes, or 3 rounded	*1 cup diced celery*
dessertspoons, gelatine	*1 green capsicum, chopped*
½ cup chopped shallots	*1 small jar stuffed olives,*
3 tablespoons raw or brown	*sliced*
sugar	*Salt and pepper*

Soften the gelatine in 1½ cups of the tomato juice. Put the remainder of the juice into a saucepan with the shallots, basil, sugar, and lemon juice. Season with salt and pepper. Bring to the boil, and simmer for a few minutes. Remove from the stove and stir in the dissolved gelatine, then the mayonnaise, celery, capsicum, and olives. Put in a cool place, and when beginning to set pour into a rinsed-out mould. Chill in the refrigerator. Serves 8.

FISH ROE ENTRÉE

½ lb. soft roes	Breadcrumbs
Plain flour	Butter
2 teaspoons basil	Salt and pepper
¼ pint cream	

Roll the roes in seasoned plain flour and lay them in a buttered ovenproof dish. Sprinkle with the basil, add the cream, top with breadcrumbs, and dot with butter. Bake in a moderate oven (350°F.) for 10 to 15 minutes. Serve hot.

BAY LEAVES

Leaves from the Bay Tree (*Laurus nobilis*) are almost an everyday ingredient in cooking, but there is hardly any mention of the tree in gardening books or catalogues. They are not easy to obtain, and yet quite apart from their aromatic and useful leaves, the bay grows into a most attractive tree. The shape is regular and compact, and the leaves have a pleasing appearance standing neatly erect and green upon the branches. These were the leaves that were fashioned into the victor's laurel wreath of the ancients.

Doctor William Turner, a sixteenth century physician, observes that "when they are casten into the fyre they crake wonderfully". And Nicholas Culpeper in the seventeenth century wrote that "neither witch nor devil, thunder nor lightning, will hurt a man where a bay tree is".

Look after your bay tree; it is a cheerful sight when healthy, but depressing when neglected. When grown in a tub it is most ornamental. Do not let it dry out, and top-dress occasionally with well-decayed manure or bone dust.

Either pick the leaves straight from the tree and use them fresh, or, if preferred, they may be dried. This is simply done by leaving them in a cool, airy place for a few days and then putting them in an airtight jar.

A bay leaf is used in a bouquet of herbs, which comprises a sprig each of thyme and parsley, and a bay leaf. Sometimes these are tied together in a muslin bag and removed before serving the dish in which they have been cooking.

It is a good idea to put a bay leaf in a casserole or stew, or when boiling pickled pork or corned beef. Bay leaves are used, also, in the making of pot-pourri.

WELSH STEW

My mother's recipe for Welsh stew, given to her by her mother, is succulent with meat and gravy, and fragrant with thyme and bay leaves. The stock may be made with beef cubes.

Cut 2 lb. beef into neat pieces and put in a casserole with 1½ pints stock. Bring to the boil, then simmer for ¾ hour. Add the white part of a bunch of leeks, well washed and cut up, a turnip cut into dice, 2 bay leaves, a spray of thyme, season with salt and pepper, and add a lump of sugar. Let all stew gently for about 1 hour. Serve in the casserole.

FISH SPECIAL

Another excellent dish from my mother's recipe book.

Roll fillets of fish prettily and place them in a buttered fireproof dish with one or two bay leaves. Over the fillets pour a glass of white wine and then sprinkle them with a layer of chopped chives or shallots. Add a few more pieces of butter and cook in a closed dish long and slowly. If allowed to get cold, the fish will be surrounded by a rich jelly.

RICE AND TREACLE PUDDING

Here is a plain but nourishing milk pudding from the family recipe book. It is popular with children.

In an ovenproof dish blend together 2 scant tablespoons rice and 1 tablespoon golden syrup. Gradually incorporate 1 pint milk. Dot with butter, and lay a bay leaf on top. Bake in a slow oven (275°F.) for about 1½ hours. May be eaten hot or cold, with cream.

STEAK CASSEROLE WITH BAY LEAVES
AND PICKLED WALNUTS

1 *lb. steak*	1 *glass red wine or stock*
4 *pickled walnuts*	1 *finely sliced onion*
2 *bay leaves*	1 *finely sliced tomato*
2 *tablespoons flour*	*Salt, pepper and sugar*

Cut steak into pieces and roll well in the flour. Put in layers in a casserole dish the steak, bay leaves, onion, tomatoes, pickled walnuts, salt, pepper and sugar to taste. (Most cooks know that sugar used sparingly helps to bring out the flavour in food.) Lastly, sprinkle any left-over flour into the casserole and pour over the wine or stock. Cover and cook in a medium oven for 2 hours.

STUFFED CABBAGE LEAVES

The following recipe for stuffed cabbage leaves is sufficient for four people, allowing two rolls for each person. The bay leaves wonderfully impart their individual aromatic flavour to the cabbage.

1 *cabbage*	1 *breakfast cup stock*
1 *lb. minced steak*	2 *or 3 bay leaves*
1 *chopped onion*	1 *small teaspoon crushed*
¾ *cup cooked rice*	*coriander seeds*

Cut leaves carefully from the cabbage and select the most suitable for rolling the meat mixture in. Trim, put in boiling water and cook for 7 minutes. Drain in a colander.

Fry the onion in a little shortening until soft, and put in a bowl with the minced steak and rice. Season with salt and pepper, add the coriander seeds and mix well. Put a good tablespoon of this mixture onto each cabbage leaf, roll up neatly and place the rolls in a casserole dish with the bay leaves. Pour in the stock, cover and simmer gently in the oven for 45 minutes. Lift out the stuffed cabbage leaves carefully, arrange on a dish, and keep hot while the stock is thickened on the stove with a little blended cornflour.

Pour the liquid over the cabbage rolls and sprinkle them with finely chopped parsley. Serve with thick slices of crusty French bread.

BERGAMOT

Bergamot (*Monarda didyma*) is a perennial and is one of the most scented of all herbs. The leaves and the flowers have a delicious fragrance which bees love, and it is sometimes known as bee balm.

This herb originated in North America, and received its botanical name from Nicolas Monardes, a Spanish physician who discovered it in the sixteenth century.

There are several varieties of *Monarda*, all popular in herbaceous borders, and bearing pale blue, pink, mauve or scarlet flowers. It is the latter, Cambridge Scarlet, which is the most popular. It grows to 4 feet in the right position, and being similar to the mint family it is happiest in a shady, rather moist position.

After flowering it dies right down and should be cut to the ground, when new leaves soon appear. The clump must be watered well in dry weather or it will die right out.

With the coming of spring and warmer weather the flower stalks rapidly begin to grow taller every day. At this time a dressing of well-decayed poultry manure helps growth, and in early summer the wonderful heads of scarlet pom-poms begin to bloom. These are full of honey, and are edible. A tossed green salad with shredded bergamot flowers added at the last not only delights the eye, but tastes excellent too. The flavour is not cloying or sweet, but delicately pungent.

The young leaves are also added to a salad, and they

impart an elusive flavour to cooking. They combine particularly well with pork, having something of the pungency of sage, and yet the scent of rosemary as well.

It is interesting to know that oil of bergamot does not come from this plant, but from a citrus tree, the bergamot orange (*Citrus bergamia*). The flavour is similar, which is the reason for this herb's everyday name.

PORK SAUSAGES WITH APPLE AND BERGAMOT

1½ lb. good pork sausages	2 cloves garlic
2 large, sliced cooking apples	1 tablespoon chopped bergamot leaves
1 oz. butter or margarine	Flour, cinnamon, salt and pepper
1 cup water or stock	
1 sliced onion	

Fry the apple (the peel may be left on for added flavour), onion and garlic in the shortening until soft, and remove from the pan. Roll the sausages in flour and fry until brown.

Place in alternate layers in a casserole dish the apple, onion and garlic mixture, the sausages, bergamot leaves, salt, pepper and a light dusting of cinnamon. Pour over the stock or water, cover and simmer for 1½ hours.

BERGAMOT SALAD AS AN ACCOMPANIMENT TO BRAWN

1 large or medium lettuce	3 bergamot flower heads
1 dessertspoon young bergamot leaves	4 hard-boiled eggs
	French dressing

Wash the lettuce and dry it thoroughly. A good idea is to do this some hours before needing it, and then put it in a covered dish in the refrigerator, it is then cool and crisp when wanted.

Wash the young bergamot leaves which may be left whole, but if possible do not wash the flowers as some of the scent is then lost.

Rub a wooden bowl with a clove of garlic, put in the torn lettuce leaves, bergamot leaves and sliced hard-boiled eggs.

Add the French dressing (1 tablespoon herb vinegar to 3 tablespoons olive or peanut oil, salt, pepper and a little sugar) and toss well. At the last tear the heads of the bergamot flowers into the salad, toss again and serve.

OSWEGO TEA

A famous refreshing tea was made from the bergamot leaves in Oswego, America, known as Oswego tea. During hot weather a few leaves, either fresh or dried, may be added when infusing ordinary package tea, and will be found refreshing and beneficial.

BERGAMOT SAUCE

1 tablespoon chopped shallots
1 oz. butter or margarine
1 wineglass white wine
Juice of ½ lemon

1 dessertspoon flour
1 dessertspoon chopped bergamot leaves
Salt and pepper

Melt the shortening and fry the shallots until soft, add the flour and stir until blended, then slowly add the wine and lemon juice. When thickened stir in the bergamot leaves, salt and pepper, and cook for a little longer. Serve hot. This is delicious with roast pork.

BORAGE

Borage (*Borago officinalis*) was esteemed more highly once than it is now. It was firmly believed that a conserve of the flowers drove away melancholy and made people merry and glad. Although it is possibly a flight of fancy to think so, perhaps there is an unknown alchemy in the plant that does do this, as all parts of this herb were known to be beneficial. The leaves, besides being a pot herb and used in salads, were also an ingredient in a "cosmetic bath", which was not only a bath to cleanse, but to strengthen the body and beautify the skin.

Borage is also one of the bee plants, and the young leaves are excellent in fruit drinks and claret cup, having a distinct cucumber flavour.

Once the seed is sown in the spring and the plant is established, there will always be borage in the garden, and although an annual, it often flowers right through the winter. It is a charming, little plant growing so demurely the blue head slightly bowed like that of some medieval lady.

The flowers are five-pointed Madonna-blue stars, the colour often used by old masters to paint the robes of Christ's mother. This is the flower featured in old needlework, and it would be delightful to see it come back into favour. Humble though it is, it has the everlasting appeal of all humble things. There is also a rare white-flowering variety.

The method for crystallizing borage flowers, as described in the following paragraph, is the same as for violets, mint leaves, carnation petals and tiny whole rosebuds. Rose petals may be preserved in this way too, or in the alternative way described in the section on Roses. It is simple and interesting to do. It is always a joy when the flowers are ready to pack into their separate jars and are put on a shelf to catch a stray glint of sunlight. They are much too pretty to shut away in a dark cupboard. The combination of glass, sunlight and glistening flower preserved in its true colour has a fascination that no bought confectionary ever has. It is wise to keep an eye open for the right kind of jar. A suggestion is to start a collection of old apothecary jars, or the glass-stoppered ones on a fairly long stem still sometimes found in sweet shops. A helpful hint is to buy a Fahrenheit thermometer for gauging the heat of the candying liquid.

CRYSTALLIZED FLOWERS

The quantity of sugar and water needed for crystallizing 2 heaped tablespoons of borage flowers or 1 bunch of large violets, is 1 lb. of castor sugar and 1 cup of water.

Put the sugar and water in a saucepan over a steady heat and bring to the boil. Have the thermometer ready standing in a jug of hot water. Lift out and stand it in the saucepan until the syrup reaches 240 degrees. Put the thermometer back into the hot water and drop the dry flowers into the syrup, about 1 dozen at a time. Boil at 240 degrees or a little more for 1 minute. Lift out the flowers with a perforated spoon and lay them carefully on a sheet of aluminium foil. Place in a slightly warmed oven and leave to cool, turning once during the process.

Instead of throwing the left-over syrup away it is a good idea to use it in a caramel custard.

CARAMEL CUSTARD

Boil the syrup further until it turns to caramel, then pour into a fireproof dish turning it quickly to cover the bottom and sides. Make a custard with 2 eggs, 1 tablespoon of sugar, and ¾ pint of milk, and pour onto the caramel. Stand in a baking dish of water and cook in a moderate oven until set. It may be served chilled and topped with whipped cream decorated with crystallized flowers.

A COSMETIC BATH

(From "The Toilet of Flora" in *The Scented Garden*, by E. S. Rohde.)

Take 2 lb. of barley or bean-meal, 8 lb. of bran, and a few handfuls of borage leaves. Boil these ingredients in a sufficient quantity of spring water. Nothing cleanses and softens the skin like this bath.

Seafood Salad (p.41).

CHERVIL

Chervil (*Anthriscus cerefolium*) is a small, twelve-inch-high biennial herb with delicate fernlike leaves. Its rather nondescript appearance is misleading as it has great culinary value, and you will find that you can never grow enough of this plant. It is grown successfully in semi-shade in summer, but it does like the winter sun, a factor which presents a problem. If it is planted where annual herbs will protect it through the hot months, by the time winter comes the annuals are out of the way and it then benefits from the sunshine.

Always pick the leaves from the outside as with parsley, allowing it to keep on growing from the centre.

This herb is particularly suitable for growing in a pot or trough. A good spot is the kitchen window-sill where it is within easy reach to pick and cut up for salads, mashed potato, and especially scrambled egg, when its nearness is appreciated for early breakfasts.

The leaves have a fresh yet spicy taste, and although it certainly does not take the place of parsley, it may, with great advantage, be used instead, adding a different flavour to familiar food. It is excellent with omelettes and in soups. Other suggestions are:

A tossed French salad with as much chopped chervil as you can spare sprinkled on the top before serving.

Diced cold potato mixed together with a light mayonnaise dressing and a generous amount of chervil.

Iced tomato soup garnished with thin slices of lemon and finely chopped chervil.

39

Fish Special (p.31).

Haricot beans served piping hot with a piquant sauce, and chervil added at the last.

Nicholas Culpeper aptly describes chervil in his *Complete Herbal* written in the seventeenth century:

"The garden chervil doth at first somewhat resemble parsley, but after it is better grown the leaves are cut in and jagged, resembling hemlock, being a little hairy, and of a whitish green colour, sometimes turning reddish in the summer, with the stalks also; it riseth a little above half a foot high, bearing white flowers in spiked tufts, which turn into long and round seeds pointed at the ends, and blackish when they are ripe . . ."

HARICOT BEANS WITH TOMATOES

This is excellent in the winter when fresh vegetables are often scarce and is quite sufficient on its own with the main meat course.

1 *lb. haricot beans*	2 *crushed cloves garlic*
1 *lb. tomatoes*	1 *dessertspoon brown sugar*
4 *shallots*	2 *tablespoons chervil*
4 *oz. butter or margarine*	*Salt and pepper*

Pour boiling water over the beans and soak overnight. Simmer in salted water until soft (about 1½ hours). Drain.

Wash the shallots and cut them up finely leaving as much of the green part as possible for colour and flavour. Put them with the garlic into a frying pan with the melted shortening. Simmer gently until soft. Peel and chop up the tomatoes and with the sugar, salt and pepper add to the frying pan. Cook a little longer, then pour the puree onto the beans and heat through. Just before serving stir in the chervil.

To vary, emulate the famous dish cassoulet, which originates from the rich farming country of south-west France, by adding to the beans ½ lb. fried, lean bacon cut into pieces, or 1 lb. of sliced garlic sausage, pour the mixture into a casserole, top with buttered breadcrumbs and brown slowly in the oven.

POTATO SOUP

1 lb. potatoes
1 onion
Chervil
1 pint stock or water

1 dessertspoon flour
  blended with milk
Little cream
Salt and pepper

Wash and slice the potato and onion, and simmer on the stove in the liquid until the vegetables are soft.

Rub through a sieve and return to the stove with the blended flour. Bring to the boil, and pour into hot soup plates. Add thin cream, fried *croûtons* and 1 teaspoon chopped chervil to each serving.

SPINACH SOUP

2 pints beef stock
1 pint cooked spinach,
  sieved or put through
  a blender

One or more 4-minute
  eggs for each person
A little cream
Chervil
Salt and pepper

Put the puréed spinach into a saucepan with the beef stock. Heat, adding salt and pepper to taste. Have ready the eggs which have been boiled and shelled. Serve the hot soup in individual bowls with a whole egg, a dessertspoon of cream, and a generous sprinkling of chervil.

SEAFOOD SALAD

3 cups fish, cooked and
  flaked
1 cup shelled prawns
1 bottle oysters, drained
1 dessertspoon chopped
  chives (or 2 dessert-
  spoons chopped shallots)
2 tomatoes, peeled and diced

1 cucumber, peeled and
  diced
½ cup mayonnaise
1 tablespoon lemon juice
1 tablespoon thick cream
Chervil
Salt and pepper

Toss all ingredients together (except the chervil) and chill in the refrigerator. Serve in a bowl lined with crisp lettuce leaves, strewing the top until green with the chervil.

This makes a refreshing accompaniment to a main dish. Slice 2 peeled and stoned avocadoes lengthwise into slender pieces. Marinate in lemon juice seasoned with salt and freshly ground pepper. To serve, sprinkle with plenty of chervil and arrange on a bed of cracked ice.

CHICORY

Chicory (*Cichorium intybus*), or succory as it was once called, is regarded more as a vegetable or pot herb, although it is delicious when a tablespoon of the finely shredded leaves are added to a lettuce salad. The leaves have a slightly bitter yet pleasant taste, and are esteemed for their health-giving properties.

Culpeper says of it: "A handful of the leaves or roots, boiled in wine or water, and drank fasting, drives forth choleric and phlegmatic humours."

The plant can grow to over six feet high, and in the autumn the china-blue flowers are carried on long spires, making a welcome show of colour in the herb garden at this time of year.

As well as having medicinal uses, the roots are dried and ground to mix with coffee, and may be boiled like parsnips and eaten as a vegetable.

Plant the seed in the spring and give this large plant plenty of room to grow.

CHICORY AND EGGS

This is an up-to-date version of an old recipe of three hundred years ago.

Blanch chicory leaves for 5 minutes in boiling water. Drain and squeeze out the moisture. Cut them with a knife and put in a saucepan with a little stock and a bunch of chopped savory herbs (marjoram, parsley and thyme for instance) and simmer for ½ hour. Thicken with a little blended corn-flour and turn onto a serving dish. Keep hot while poach-

43

ing the eggs to lay upon the cooked chicory. Serve at once.

CHICORY SALAD

1 *lettuce*	4 *peeled tomatoes cut into*
1 *chicory leaf*	*quarters*
1 *doz. stoned black olives*	1 *tablespoon chopped*
8 *anchovies*	*chervil and chives in*
4 *hard-boiled eggs*	*equal parts*
1 *cup diced celery*	*French dressing*

Chop the fresh, dry chicory leaf and put with the torn-up lettuce in a bowl that has been rubbed with a cut clove of garlic. Add all ingredients except the herbs, anchovies and hard-boiled eggs and toss well. Arrange the halved eggs with an anchovy on each one on top of the salad, and sprinkle with herbs. Serve with cold meat and French bread for lunch, or alfresco on a hot summer night.

CHIVES

Chives (*Allium schoenoprasum*) belongs to the same family as the onion, leek, garlic and shallot. The thin, grass-like leaves have a delicate taste of onion, and are generally used to flavour cream cheese, salads and omelettes.

Chives makes an attractive border, the flowers are decorative, looking like little mauve pincushions, and are charming in a mixed posy.

If both the leaves and the flowers are picked continually, the plant is improved by growing more vigorously and having a better flavour. Chives may suddenly die out and disappear, so divide the bulbs in the autumn to prevent overcrowding, water them in dry weather and top-dress twice a year with old poultry humus.

If raising the plant from seed, sow in the spring. It grows successfully on a kitchen window-sill, and has the added advantage of being within easy reach when needed.

Chives and cream cheese have an affinity. Chop the chives finely and mash them into the cream cheese with salt, pepper, a little cream and a squeeze of lemon juice. Spread on savouries and in sandwiches or pat into a mound in the centre of a serving dish and surround with biscuits; supply a knife and let everyone help themselves to this savoury mixture either as a before-dinner appetizer, or to eat afterwards.

Another suggestion is to add a tablespoon of chopped chives to mashed potato, particularly when accompanying grilled chops, steak, or crumbed cutlets. In scrambled eggs, or in an omelette, chives are equally delicious. The uses of this herb are many and varied, especially to the imaginative cook.

Cucumber and chives combine well, and the first recipe to follow—Creamed Cucumber—is excellent.

CREAMED CUCUMBER

2 *green cucumbers, or*	1 *cup white sauce*
6 *apple cucumbers*	*Salt and pepper*
1 *tablespoon chopped chives*	

Peel the cucumbers, cut into cubes, put into boiling water and cook a few minutes. Drain. Make a white sauce with 1½ tablespoons of butter, 2 level tablespoons of flour and 1 cup of milk. Stir in the cucumber, chives, salt and pepper. Heat through and serve hot.

FRENCH OMELETTE WITH CHIVES

Those who own a correct omelette pan, heavy with a flat bottom and shallow with sloping sides, are fortunate; however a successful omelette may still be made in an ordinary frying pan. Experienced cooks say that one omelette should never contain more than six eggs, and in some recipe books there are whole pages devoted to the art of omelette-making. I find it easier to make several, one for each person, unless making the omelette for two people, in which case six eggs may be used.

3 eggs
1 oz. butter
Chives, salt and pepper

Dissolve the butter over a medium heat. Meanwhile, break the eggs into a bowl and whisk well but lightly. Season with salt and pepper, add two tiny cubes of butter and the chives.

When the butter is sizzling gently, see that it is distributed evenly over the pan, and pour in the eggs. With a knife quickly lift up the sides of the omelette all round the pan allowing the mixture to run underneath. Do this several times, and cut it once across the middle. The bottom of the omelette should be set and a golden brown, the top creamy and not quite cooked. Lift the omelette with an egg slice, fold it over and slide it onto a hot plate and serve immediately.

FISH PIE WITH HERBS

3 *cups cooked flaked fish*
1½ *cups white sauce*
1 *tablespoon chopped chives*
1 *dessertspoon chopped parsley*
1 *dessertspoon chopped walnuts*
Salt, pepper, grated nutmeg

Stir the fish into the white sauce. Season with salt, pepper and nutmeg. Put into a fireproof dish and top with herbs and walnuts. Brown in a medium oven and serve with slices of lemon and very thin brown bread and butter.

CORIANDER

Coriander (*Coriandrum sativum*) is an annual and is grown for its aromatic seeds which must be allowed to ripen before using, as they are unpleasant when fresh.

Sow the seed in the spring, when the plant will soon grow to about two feet. After flowering, collect the seeds and allow to dry, or leave to ripen on the plant, but do not wait too long otherwise they will all drop off.

Coriander is one of our more musical words, bringing to the imagination medieval gardens where the names of flowers were strung together like garlands; coriander, cumin and southernwood; rue, elecampane and tansy; costmary, cowslips and gilliflowers. It also conjures up the richness of the East and the pageantry of the Old Testament, of gold, frankincense and myrrh. It is as old as the Bible, and is mentioned in Exodus, ch. 16, v. 31:

"And the house of Israel called the name thereof Manna: and it was like coriander seed, white; and the taste of it was like wafers made with honey."

The fragrant seeds are an ingredient in both curry powder and pot-pourri, and are often added to give a spicy flavour to food. A teaspoon of crushed seeds gives a subtle undertone to casseroles and soups.

BAKED VEAL CHOPS

Pound 2 cloves of garlic and 2 teaspoons coriander seed together, and mix with breadcrumbs. Dip chops in flour, egg and seasoned breadcrumbs, put in a baking dish with a little fat and the grated rind of $\frac{1}{2}$ lemon. Cook in a moderate oven until brown and crisp.

Crumbed bananas may, with advantage, be added to the baking dish 15 minutes before serving.

SPICED TEA CAKE

1 *tablespoon butter*	1 *peeled thinly sliced apple*
½ *cup sugar*	1 *dessertspoon pounded*
1 *egg*	*coriander seed*
1 *cup milk*	*A little sugar and nutmeg*
1 *cup S.R. flour*	

Cream the butter and sugar. Add the egg and beat well. Gently fold in the sifted flour and milk alternately.

Smear a cake tin with butter and then a dusting of flour. (This prevents the cake from sticking.) Lay the sliced apple in the bottom of the tin, and sprinkle with sugar, nutmeg and pounded coriander seed. Pour the batter over and bake in a moderate oven until cooked, about ½ hour. Carefully loosen the cake from the sides of the tin, and turn onto a plate or wire-cooler. It is delicious when hot, but may be eaten cold with thick cream.

MARMALADE FLAVOURED WITH CORIANDER

4 *oranges*	4 *lb. sugar*
2 *lemons*	1 *tablespoon crushed*
6 *cups water*	*coriander seed*

Cut up the oranges and lemons and soak in water for 12 hours. Bring to the boil and put in the coriander seed tied in a muslin bag. When the peel is tender slowly add the warmed sugar, and boil until the mixture jellies. Remove the muslin bag before putting the marmalade in jars.

The coriander seed will impart a spicy fragrance to the usually prosaic marmalade.

DILL

Dill (*Anethum graveolens*) is a tall annual growing to a height of three feet and over. Its lacy leaves are delicately aromatic, and when chopped up finely they give potato salads and cucumber sandwiches an interesting new flavour.

Sow the seed in the spring after frosts, where the plants are to remain, and thin out later, leaving a foot between each. It is unwise to plant dill near fennel, for when you come to collect the seeds you will find that the mature plants are so similar in appearance and flavour that it will take time and close examination to sort them out satisfactorily. Dill is a more delicate plant in every way; the stalk is finer and the leaves have a more subtle flavour, reminiscent of carraway. Fennel is more like aniseed, and the seed-heads are smaller and not as heavy and full as dill.

Dill water is well known for soothing babies, and as early as Saxon times it was used for this purpose.

Dill pickles are a delicious and popular continental food. Dill sauce with fish is excellent, and it is also one of the herbs that may be used with advantage in scrambled eggs and mashed potatoes. The pale-yellow flower-heads, too, are pretty enough to bring inside and arrange in a mixed bowl, having an airy appearance and the simple charm of wayside flowers.

DILL PICKLES

When dill pickles are made at home in the correct way,

they are so superior to the product sold in shops that it is almost like eating a completely different food.

The crispness of the cucumbers and the subtle flavours in the brine are the outstanding qualities of home-made dill pickles (or dill cucumbers as they are sometimes called). To achieve the desired crispness of the cucumber there are certain simple, but definite rules to be followed.

First of all it is important to grow your own cucumbers so that they may be freshly picked when they are only 4 or 5 inches long, and put straight into the *coldest part of the refrigerator 24 hours* before putting them into the brine. This is the first step towards crispness.

With twelve little green cucumbers frosting under the ice trays, go into the garden and gather:

4 *sprays of dill about 6 inches long*	1 *spray of basil*
	1 *sprig of tarragon*
2 *leaves from the grape vine*	1 *tiny spike of rosemary*
	1 *sage leaf*

Then go back into the kitchen and place them in the bottom of a large saucepan, together with:

4 *cloves of garlic*	4 *to 6 crushed peppercorns*
½ *dried bay leaf*	*A few carraway seeds*
1 *dry chili*	¾ *cup salt*

Add the cucumbers and cover with *boiling water*. This is the second step that ensures crisp cucumbers. Put the lid on the saucepan and leave to cool.

When cold pour the contents into a large screwtop jar, making sure the brine covers the cucumbers. Store for about 2 weeks, and begin to use, first of all lifting any mildew off the top. Keep jar in the refrigerator once it is being used.

SCALLOPS WITH DILL

Roll 1 lb. of scallops in flour, egg and breadcrumbs, and fry in ¼ lb. of melted butter or margarine for a few minutes on either side. Put scallops in a dish and keep hot. Stir 1 good tablespoon of flour into the shortening, adding a little more if necessary, and blend well over medium heat. Pour 1 scant cup of stock or milk and 1 tablespoon sherry into the pan and stir until thick. Add 1 tablespoon of finely chopped dill, and pour the sauce over the scallops. Serve at once.

51

Cole-slaw or cabbage salad is economical to make and tasty to eat in the summer either by itself with cold meat or served with other salads; it also goes equally as well with hot food in the winter.

1 *small firm cabbage*
2 *tablespoons chopped dill*
1 *chopped green apple*

1 *breakfast cup of mayonnaise (the readymade kind sold in shops is quick and easy)*

Trim and wash the cabbage, cut it into four and shred it as thinly as possible; the finer it is cut the better it is. Put the shredded cabbage into boiling salted water and boil for 5 minutes, then tip it into a colander and run cold water over it for a few minutes. Let the cabbage drain thoroughly, shaking it occasionally. When it is quite free of water put it into a bowl with the dill and apple, pour the dressing over and mix the salad well. It may be left overnight in the refrigerator with a plate over the top to prevent any odour from the cabbage affecting other food.

FENNEL

Sweet fennel (*Foeniculum vulgare*) is a perennial, while Florence or finochio fennel (*F. vulgare dulce*) is an annual. The latter is more popular; not only are both the leaves and seeds used, but the base of the stems, which are bulbous, are either eaten raw like celery, or are gently boiled until tender and served with white sauce.

Grow Florence fennel in a sunny position and give it plenty of moisture. When the base begins to swell, cultivate and feed the soil.

In appearance fennel resembles dill, although usually not growing so high. The leaves and seeds are similar in flavour, fennel being more pungent, and distinctly reminiscent of aniseed.

There are many legends and beliefs surounding this herb, and it has been mentioned by poets and writers throughout the centuries. One of its virtues was supposed to be that of restoring eyesight, another, to reduce overweight.

The chopped leaves of fennel are used in a sauce for fish, or a sprig may be placed inside the fish when grilling or baking.

The bulbous stalk is eaten in various ways, perhaps the most tasty being a salad made of the sliced, nutty, raw fennel and a tin of asparagus, cut into rounds, tossed together with French dressing and a dessertspoon of finely chopped chervil. This is something different and delicious in the way of salads, and is excellent with cold chicken.

53

The continental vegetable markets are famous for their colourful and tempting varieties of vegetables—heaped white bunches of Florence fennel, eggplant or aubergines, green and red peppers, broccoli, globe artichokes, endives, small marrows or courgettes, and so on.

COOKED FENNEL

Pull the fennel from the ground and cut away the leafy tops (put them in the refrigerator wrapped in tin foil for using some other time), wash well and cut into pieces. Simmer gently until tender. Drain. Make a white sauce and add the cooked fennel. Heat through and stir in a dessert-spoon of chopped parsley before serving.

FENNEL CREAM SAUCE
(For fish.)

1 *cup cream*	2 *tablespoons finely*
1 *tablespoon lemon juice*	*chopped fennel*
1 *teaspoon honey*	*Salt and pepper*

Whip cream until thickened but not too fluffy, stir in the honey and lemon, blending well. Add fennel and seasoning last.

FENNEL-SEED SAUSAGE

A homemade sausage eaten cold is delicious and also nourishing, as well as being economical. With a good basic recipe, there can always be variations in the flavour and meat. For instance, 2 lb. of sausage meat could be substituted for 2 lb. of minced steak. The fennel seeds may be omitted. Garlic, onion, and parsley may all be added separately, or together. It is entirely a matter of taste. This recipe is simple, and is such a family favourite that it vanishes almost immediately.

2 *lb. minced steak*	2 *level tablespoons of*
2 *eggs*	*fennel seeds*
4 *cups soft breadcrumbs*	1 *chopped onion, salt and*
	pepper

Put the meat, breadcrumbs, fennel seeds and onion in a bowl, add the beaten eggs and mix well together. Have ready a clean floured cloth. Form the mixture into a sausage on the cloth, and roll the cloth well round, tying each end with string. Put into a large saucepan of boiling water, and boil for 2½ hours. Lift out carefully, onto a plate, unfold the cloth and slip it away from the sausage, roll in dry breadcrumbs and leave to cool.

GARLIC

Garlic (*Allium sativum*) should definitely have a place in the store cupboard, for the discreet use of this pungent herb improves many dishes. The bulb is the part that is used. This is made up of separate sections called cloves, and covered by a light skin, which is peeled before using.

Garlic was once known as a valuable medicinal herb, and today it is still highly regarded by many people for having a beneficial effect on the digestive system and for improving the complexion. There is a herb farm in England that sells garlic specially prepared in capsule form for this purpose.

If you like garlic, it is a temptation to use it quite lavishly, and to eat it raw, perhaps finely sliced on bread with cheese. This is a dangerous practice for the effects stay for a long time and is rather hard on other people! Unless contemplating a day or two of solitude, it might be wise to follow Bottom's counsel in *A Midsummer Night's Dream*, "eat no onions nor garlic, for we are to utter sweet breath". A clove of garlic rubbed round a wooden salad bowl, or garlic butter spread on a hot French loaf is usually sufficient when using it raw.

When cooked, especially for a long time, garlic imparts its fragrance to the dish, while not being in any way offensive to those who are prejudiced against it. It is astonishing how many cloves may be used in one dish, with the addition of shallots, without making it overwhelming, providing it is cooked long and slowly.

Garlic belongs to the same family as the shallot, onion, chives, leek and rocambole. Grow it in rich, friable soil, planting the cloves to a depth of 2 inches, and 6 inches apart, in May and June. Keep the bed weeded and watered. The bulbs may be lifted and stored the following January, the best of the cloves being kept on one side for planting again at the right time.

There are numerous ways of using garlic. Here are three suggestions that will be found particularly helpful.

1. When roasting lamb or mutton, especially if it seems to be a little tough, make one or two incisions in the raw meat with a knife and insert small cloves of garlic. It seems to act as a tenderizer as well as deliciously flavouring the meat.

2. Rub a small square of bread on both sides with garlic and place at the bottom of the salad bowl with the lettuce on top. By the time you come to toss it, the aroma will have penetrated the lettuce.

3. Chop 6 cloves of garlic very finely until it is almost pulp, then mash it into $\frac{1}{4}$ lb. softened butter. Spread on slices of hot crusty French bread and serve in a basket with any luncheon dish.

CASSEROLE SAUSAGES IN CIDER

8 *sausages*	1 *cup of cider*
2 *apples*	*Herbs, salt and pepper*
4 *shallots*	2 *tablespoons of flour*
2 or 3 *cloves of garlic*	

Roll the sausages well in flour and fry them lightly all over in a little clear fat. Put them in a casserole dish with layers of sliced apple, cored but not peeled, finely chopped shallots (do not discard the green part, it is edible and adds colour), finely chopped garlic and some sage and parsley. Season with salt and pepper. Add a cup of cider. Cover and cook in a medium oven for 1 hour.

I find butcher's sausages best to use, they are more meaty as a rule, making this a nourishing and savoury meal.

STUFFED STEAK ROLLS

1½ *lb. round steak*
1 *cup of stock, water or red wine*

Stuffing

1 *cup of soft breadcrumbs*
2 *rashers of bacon cut into small pieces*
2 *cloves of finely chopped garlic*
1 *dessertspoon each of chopped onion, celery and parsley*
1 *tablespoon of melted butter*

Cut the steak into strips. Combine the stuffing and spread on the strips. Roll up and secure with wooden toothpicks. Roll lightly in flour and brown in a little shortening. Add the liquid, and simmer in a medium oven for 2 hours.

LAVENDER

Nearly every garden has at least one lavender bush. It is not surprising that this beautifully scented small shrub has kept its popularity throughout the centuries, long before the Christian era up to the present time.

There is no scent quite like lavender, each spray containing the warm, sweet smell of summer. Shakespeare, in *The Winter's Tale*, calls it "hot lavender":

> *Here's flowers for you;*
> *Hot lavender, mints, savory, marjoram;*
> *The marigold, that goes to bed wi' the sun,*
> *And with him rises weeping . . .*

Even on the bleakest winter's day, when a dried lavender flower or a lavender sachet is held and inhaled for a moment, a picture immediately forms of long, drowsy days, humming bees and a glowing tapestry of flowers in the garden.

Lavender is a *xerophyte*, which means that is especially adapted for living in dry conditions. The grey leaves indicate this quality, the greyness really being a mass of tiny white hairs, which are there to hold moisture within the plant. This is a planting guide to many grey-leaved plants, sage being another, also the old-fashioned herbaceous border favourite lychnis, although if you were to snap any of these leaves in half you would find that they are green inside. Do not feel that rich soil will prevent a lavender bush from growing well. As long as it is well-drained and not in clay soil, it will flourish.

Working a little lime around the roots will benefit the plant under these conditions.

Pot-pourri is not complete without lavender, which retains its perfume long after the other flowers have faded, with the exception of rosemary. These two plants have strong, natural aromatic oils, which are known and valued by chemical firms and are extracted for use in commerce.

The two common varieties are *Lavandula dentata,* and *L. vera.* The first is generally known as French lavender, and grows into a large bushy shrub with grey, serrated leaves and pale mauve blossoms. It likes a sunny position and light sandy soil, and is almost always in bloom, its main flush being in the winter. It is recommended to use as a hedge, and grows exceptionally well on a stone wall.

L. vera is the English lavender, and there are other varieties closely resembling it known as *L. officinalis* and *L. spica.* It is a small-growing shrub, its smooth grey leaves are narrow and pointed, and the flowers which bloom in summer grow in long spikes of deep mauve. The scent of English lavender is incomparable, and for a low hedge it is ideal.

L. stoechas is also known as French lavender, and was once called by the quaint old name of sticadove. This dwarf variety is not often seen. It blooms in the spring and is worth growing for this reason and for its rich, purple flower-heads, similar in form to *L. dentata.* There is also a white flowering lavender, *L. officinalis alba,* which is rare and very sweet.

Any leaf or flower that comes from a lavender bush should never be wasted. When blooms that have been picked, are spent, they may be tied in bunches to perfume drawers and linen cupboards, or added to the pot-pourri bowl, together with the aromatic leaves. Lavender should be pruned after flowering, to ensure a healthy well-shaped shrub. The prunings, of course, should not be wasted either. When lavender cuttings are put in sand, two-thirds of each cutting should be stripped of its leaves; these leaves are gathered up and put straight into the large earthenware jar that always contains pot-pourri.

Long ago lavender was used not only for making scented articles, but in confectionery, cooking and in medicine. There are delightful old recipes for lavender wine, lavender sugar, lavender water, lavender tea, the distilling of lavender for the volatile oil, as well as directions for making lavender fans, lavender bags and lavender quilted into caps. One charming idea that could be used today is to spear sweets and small pieces of fruit with spikes of English lavender.

AN AROMATIC BATH

This is a simplified version of an old recipe:
Boil for 5 minutes, in a sufficient quantity of water, one or all of the following plants: bay leaves, thyme, rosemary, marjoram, lavender, wormwood, pennyroyal, balm and eau-de-Cologne mint. Strain and add a little brandy. Shake the required quantity into a hot bath.

LAVENDER SUGAR

In the seventeenth century a favourite confectionery was Lavender Sugar, made by beating lavender flowers into three times their weight in sugar. If you put two or three lavender heads into the sugar cannister it will scent the sugar beautifully.

LAVENDER WATER WITHOUT DISTILLATION

(From "The Toilet of Flora" in *The Scented Garden*, by E. S. Rohde.)

If you would have speedily, without the trouble of distillation, a water impregnated with the flavour of Lavender, put two or three drops of Oil of Spike, and a lump of Sugar, into a pint of clear Water, or Spirit of Wine, and shake them well together in a glass phial, with a narrow neck. This Water, though not distilled, is very fragrant.

If you desire lavender vinegar to give a subtle fragrance to salads, steep lavender heads in 1 pint of white vinegar in a glass container on a sunny shelf for 2 weeks. Strain and use.

Although the little-known plant often called lavender cotton or French lavender (*Santolina chamae cyparissus*) does not belong to the lavender family at all, it may be included here to bring up the rear of the lavenders. With its fragrant foliage, resembling delicate grey coral, and round yellow flowers, it is a decorative and charming addition to any garden. It likes to grow in the same type of soil as the lavenders, light and well drained in a sunny position where it will attain a height of three feet with a spreading habit. Do not prune heavily.

Sprays of this herb were once laid in drawers to keep away moths, and oil for perfume from the plant is used industrially. The leaves and flowers are valuable in pot-pourri, adding colour as well as scent.

MARJORAM

There are many different species of the valuable culinary herb marjoram, the most popular variety being the sweet marjoram (*Origanum majorana*).

Marjoram is a perennial and very easy to grow. Sow the seed in spring, or propagate by root division. It likes a sunny, well-drained position, and if cut back after flowering, will grow into a healthy, shrubby plant about two feet high. When winter frosts have driven basil from the herb garden, marjoram comes into its own. It is difficult to choose between these two herbs for savoury flavour. Marjoram is more subtle, not giving its aroma as freely as basil. A light touch of the hand, or spray from the hose will release the fragrance of basil, but you must pick a stalk of marjoram, when the soft and scented leaves will tempt you to nibble and enjoy their pungency.

Marjoram may be used in a number of ways and it is wise to have more than one bush growing. Delicious brown-bread sandwiches are made with marjoram leaves spread thickly on a bed of cream cheese. Use the leaves in herb scones (a family favourite), in salads, omelettes and sauces, in vinegars, sweet bags and pot-pourri. There is also the customary bouquet of herbs for flavouring soups and stews, in which thyme, parsley, marjoram and a bay leaf are usually recommended.

Although marjoram was once used medicinally for a number of complaints—from digestive disorders to curing toothache—it was also highly valued as a "strewing" herb on the floors of houses.

Marjoram is more pungent, perhaps, when dried than it is fresh. Although fresh herbs are probably superior, it is sometimes more convenient to use dried herbs, even when the former is available. When marjoram is just beginning to flower, cut some of it for drying, and proceed as described earlier for drying herbs.

COTTAGE PIE

This familiar dish is sometimes called Shepherd's Pie, another homely old name, indicating the popularity of the dish over the years. It consists of minced meat with a topping of mashed potato, and is always appetizing whether perfectly plain with only the addition of gravy and a little onion to the meat, or flavoured in a number of different ways. It is important to have the mashed potato crisp and golden. This recipe is for fresh meat, but it could be made with minced left-over meat and a cup of gravy, omitting the cup of liquid and the flour.

4 *shallots*	1 *cup stock or water*
2 *rashers bacon*	1 *tablespoon marjoram*
1 *clove garlic*	*leaves*
1 *lb. minced steak*	*Salt and pepper*
1 *tablespoon flour*	1 *lb. mashed potatoes*

Wash and cut up the shallots, using as much of the green part as possible. Chop the garlic very finely. Cut the bacon into small pieces. Melt some oil in a large frying pan and cook these ingredients until soft. Add marjoram leaves and the minced steak. Press down with a fork, and brown all over, mixing the contents of the pan well together. Add the flour, cook a little longer, then pour in the liquid. Season. Turn into an oven-proof dish and top with creamy mashed potato. A tablespoon of nutty sesame seeds and pieces of butter spread over the potato before putting it in the oven is excellent. Bake in a medium oven for $\frac{3}{4}$ hour. If the top is not browned enough turn on the griller for a few minutes before serving.

While picking a bunch of parsley one day, a neighbour gave me this delicious recipe for using it in scones to put on top of a bubbling casserole or stew, half an hour before serving. In fact any savoury herb may be used that seems best suited to the dish it is accompanying, and in winter it is particularly nourishing. When roasting pork, mix rosemary leaves (cut up finely with the kitchen scissors) into the scones and bake on a tray in the oven. Served dry like this they are appropriate with a rich meat.

1 *cup S.R. flour*   2 *tablespoons chopped marjoram*
2 *oz. butter*   *leaves*
                          Pinch salt and a little cold water

Sift flour and salt. Rub in the butter. Add marjoram and enough cold water to make a stiff dough. Stir quickly and lightly with a knife and then pat out on the table with your hand. Cut into squares and use straight away, or wrap in tin foil and put in the refrigerator until needed.

SUMMER VEGETABLE TART

Marjoram is used in a lightly scented seasoning for this tart, which may be eaten at luncheon or supper or taken on a picnic.

Rich short-crust pastry: Sift 1½ cups self-raising flour and a pinch of salt into a bowl, rub in ¼ lb. butter until the mixture is crumbly, add ¼ cup very cold water and a squeeze of lemon juice, and mix to a dry dough.

Filling: 1 cup cooked peas, 2 cooked carrots finely sliced, 1 cup cooked potatoes finely sliced, 2 tablespoons chopped shallots, 3 eggs, ½ cup cream, 2 teaspoons marjoram, some salt and pepper.

Roll the pastry out thinly and line a buttered 8-inch shallow pie-dish with it. Prick the pastry all over, and fill with the vegetables, arranging them attractively. Mix the eggs, cream, and marjoram together, seasoning with salt and pepper, and pour carefully over the vegetables. Bake in a moderate oven (375°F.) until set—about 30 minutes. Serve the tart warm or cold, decorated with a few fresh marjoram leaves.

3 doz. oysters, drained
2 heaped tablespoons finely
  chopped shallots
2 oz. butter
1 cup white wine
1 dessertspoon lemon
  juice

2 teaspoons marjoram
1 scant tablespoon plain
  flour
1 cup thin cream
Salt and pepper
Ground nutmeg

Soften the shallots in butter without browning. Add the wine, lemon juice, and marjoram, season with salt and pepper, and simmer over low heat until reduced a little. Mix the flour and cream together, add to the sauce and stir until thickened. Remove from heat, stir the oysters into the sauce, and spoon into ramekins or scallop shells. Sprinkle lightly with nutmeg, put into the oven, and heat through for 5 to 8 minutes. Serve hot with small squares of brown bread-and-butter.

Whitebait, scallops, or sliced fish fillets may be used in place of oysters. Sauce Bercy may also be served over asparagus, sliced avocado pear, sautéed mushrooms or with delicately textured grilled meat.

VEAL IN APPLE JUICE

1½ lb. veal steak
One 15½-oz. tin, or 2¼ cups,
  apple juice
2 tablespoons plain flour
2 teaspoons marjoram
2 teaspoons mustard seed

1 crumbled bay-leaf
1 onion, finely chopped
1 clove of garlic, finely
  chopped
A few peppercorns
Salt

Cut the veal into strips, roll them in flour and place them in an ovenproof dish. Sprinkle with half each of the marjoram, mustard seed, crumbled bay-leaf, onion, garlic, and peppercorns, with a little salt. Repeat, then pour the apple juice over. Cover, and bake in a moderate oven (350°F.) for 1 to 1½ hours.

BURNING STEAK

This way of preparing fillet steak is different, and fun to do. The flavour of the burnt brandy, and the aromatic

66

marjoram leaves sprinkled over the cooked steak, makes it a meal to be enjoyed.

4 *pieces of fillet steak*   2 *tablespoons finely chopped*
½ *cup brandy*   *marjoram leaves*
                       Butter, salt and pepper

Melt butter in a heavy frying pan and put in the steaks. Let them sizzle, turn them over and cook a little longer. Pour the brandy over and set alight. When the flames have died down put the steaks on a hot dish. Pour liquor from the pan over, dust with salt and freshly ground pepper, and top with the marjoram leaves.

POTATO PIE

If you decide to serve one vegetable with a meal, potatoes with marjoram is quite substantial.

1 *lb. potatoes*   2 *tablespoons marjoram leaves*
4 *shallots*   ¼ *lb. butter, salt and pepper*

Peel the potatoes and slice them thinly. Place in layers in a buttered pie dish the potatoes, marjoram leaves, pieces of butter and finely sliced shallots. Top with buttered bread-crumbs and cook slowly in a medium oven, about 1 hour.

MARJORAM VINEGAR

Fill a glass jar with marjoram leaves and pour the best white vinegar over them. Cover and leave on a sunny shelf for 2 weeks. Strain and use.

MINT

There is a bed of mint to be found in nearly every garden. No wonder it has not vanished from our daily lives as so many other herbs have done; for besides being very hardy, the delicious, piercing quality of its scent has its own appeal.

Culpeper describes a formidable number of diseases in which preparations of this herb were used medicinally. It is mentioned in the New Testament and mints are described in early English plant lists.

Mint was valued for scenting baths and to "strengthen the sinews" at the same time. It was also used as a strewing herb, in teas and in confectionery. A few sprigs of mint boiled with new potatoes is believed to make them more digestible.

There are many varieties of mint, the best known being spearmint (*Mentha spicata*). It is interesting to grow other kinds as well. Applemint (*M. rotundifolia*) which smells strongly of apples is recommended for mint sauce.

Eau-de-Cologne mint (*M. piperita citrata*), sometimes known as bergamot mint, has dark purplish leaves with an aroma definitely reminiscent of eau-de-Cologne. Put a sprig in the saucepan when cooking peas, and enjoy the scent that fills the kitchen, and at the same time delicately permeates the peas. This particular mint makes a refreshing tea on hot days.

The lower-growing peppermint or menthol (*M. piperita officinalis*) is the true Mitcham peppermint, and the oil from this plant is used commercially. A tisane made from menthol is highly esteemed for its beneficial effects when suffering from a cold.

Pennyroyal (*M. pulegium*) once valued for ridding rooms of fleas, is a pretty little edging or rockery plant with circlets of mauve flowers on miniature spires in spring. Its leaves, smelling and tasting of peppermint, are excellent when used liberally with new potatoes and butter.

The curly mint (*M. spicata crispata*) with its crinkly leaves, is used in mint sauce and is most attractive and tastes delicious when crystallized.

All the mints like fairly rich soil and plenty of water, and as they have rampant root systems, it is wise to give them room to grow. If space is limited, each variety may be confined in a chimney pot buried up to the rim in the ground. Propagate by root division, preferably in winter or spring.

It has been found that leaves from a mint plant grown in the sun have a better flavour than those from a more lush-looking plant grown in the shade; but when cultivated in full sunlight, mint must be watered more frequently. It is well worth the small amount of extra work.

Mint may be dried on racks or in bunches hung in an airy place. The leaves should then be stripped from the stems and rubbed through a fine sieve. After having been treated in this way, 7 lb. of fresh mint is reduced to about 1 lb. The flavour is much stronger than that of fresh mint, of course, and only a small amount should be used at a time.

It is in the summer that mint is really appreciated for its fresh flavour and invigorating properties. In the making of fruit drinks it is invaluable, and some dried leaves mixed with package tea are refreshing on a very hot day.

There are many well-known ways of using mint in cooking, and the following recipes contain a few additional ideas for making a wider employment of this pleasant and beneficial herb.

Mint sauce for roast lamb is made in less than a minute by putting a dessertspoon of dried mint into a small jug with sugar, vinegar, and hot water.

For a change when making mint sauce, sweeten with honey instead of sugar, and use lemon instead of vinegar, and remember there should always be lots of mint in it.

Tasty sandwiches are made with brown bread, cream cheese and finely chopped mint leaves.

Fry bananas lightly in butter with plenty of chopped-up mint to accompany crumbed cutlets.

A teaspoon or two of dried mint may be sprinkled on tomatoes just before they are grilled, fried, or baked.

Shake a little dried or chopped fresh mint into scrambled egg, mashed potato, or buttered vegetables before serving.

Mint is supposed to prevent milk from curdling. Eleanour Sinclair Rohde, in *A Garden of Herbs*, quotes this old recipe from *The Good Housewife's Handmaid*, 1588: "Mintes put into milk, it neyther suffereth the same to curde, nor to become thick, insomuch that layed in curded milke, this would bring the same thinne againe."

FRENCH-STYLE PEAS

Shell 1½ lb. fresh young peas, or use a packet (8 to 12 oz.) of good-quality frozen peas. Wash the heart of a lettuce and arrange it in a saucepan, add the peas, 1 dessertspoon chopped spring onions, 2 teaspoons dried mint, a pinch each of salt and sugar, and a few pieces of butter. Put the lid on the saucepan and place over a low heat. Shake the pan frequently at first; after a few minutes you will see that the peas are cooking in the moisture from the lettuce and the melted butter. Five to seven minutes is usually sufficient cooking time. Serve the peas and spring onions with the cooked lettuce, which is delicate and delicious.

MINT AND MARSHMALLOW CUSTARD

This simple milk pudding may be eaten either hot or cold. The marshmallows become caramelized, and the mint counteracts any tendency to over-sweetness.

With a fork beat together in an ovenproof dish 3 eggs and 1 tablespoon sugar. Gradually mix in 1 pint milk. Dust with 2 teaspoons dried mint and float about 24 marshmallows on top. Stand the dish in a shallow container of hot water, and place in a moderate oven (350°F.) to bake until set.

MINT AND CHEESE DRESSING

To make this delicious dressing for baked potatoes, take 2 teaspoons dried mint and 1 packet of cream cheese, and pound a small clove of garlic. Mix thoroughly. Wash and dry some potatoes, rub them well with vegetable oil, and bake in a hot oven (400°F.) for 1 hour. Remove the potatoes from the oven, slit the tops with a knife and squeeze their sides slightly. Spoon the cheese dressing over them and serve hot.

MINTED EGG TART

½ lb. *cream cheese*
6 *eggs*
3 *tablespoons well-chopped mint*
1 *thinly sliced cucumber with the peel left on*
Short pastry

Line a pie dish with a thin layer of short pastry (I have given a recipe for pastry in the chapter on sage), spread with cream cheese or cottage cheese which has been mashed with some top milk or cream, and cover with the cucumber. Break the eggs onto this, season with salt and pepper and strew the top with mint, using spearmint or applemint. Bake in a moderate oven until the pastry is golden and the eggs set, about ½ hour. This is particularly delicious in hot weather, eaten cold for lunch, or to take on a picnic. A glass of icy apple cider and thin slices of cold ham or veal makes an excellent accompaniment.

MINT JULEP

Wash a large bunch of mint (eau-de-Cologne mint is especially good) and put it in a basin. Bruise it and then add 1 cup of sugar, 1 tin of pineapple juice and the juice of 4 lemons. Cover and let it stand for some hours, then strain into a tall jug. Add 3 bottles of dry ginger ale, cubes of ice, thin slices of lemon and sprigs of mint. This has been a wonderful standby for luncheon on many occasions, and is preferred by many people to wine in the middle of the day.

MINT JELLY

1½ oz. gelatine
½ pint hot water
12 oz. sugar
1¼ pints white vinegar

4 tablespoons chopped mint (spearmint, apple-mint or curly mint)

Dissolve sugar in the vinegar by bringing to the boil and boil for 4 minutes. Dissolve gelatine in the hot water and add it with the mint and a pinch of salt to the vinegar. Bring it to the boil once more and remove immediately. Add a few drops of green colouring and allow to cool, stirring occasionally. When beginning to set put into small pots. Cover and keep in the refrigerator. Excellent with lamb, mutton, veal and pork as a change from mint sauce.

CRYSTALLIZED MINT LEAVES

Select the best leaves of curly mint, applemint or eau-de-Cologne mint. See that they are perfectly dry, and with a fine paint brush coat each one on both sides with a slightly beaten egg white, then dust all over with castor sugar. Put on waxed paper in a warm oven to dry, leaving the door half open. Turn occasionally. When quite dry and glistening greenly, nibble one or two and see how delicious and pepper-minty they taste. Put them away in an airtight container between layers of waxed paper and use for garnishing sweets and cakes.

PINEAPPLE COCKTAIL

1 *pineapple*
2 *tablespoons of finely chopped mint*
1 *cup of sugar*

Peel the pineapple. Stand it on a plate and slice downwards with a knife until the hard core is reached. Cut the pineapple pieces into cubes. Strain the juice into a saucepan with the sugar and mint and bring to the boil and simmer for a few minutes. Pour back onto the pineapple. Chill in the refrigerator and serve as an appetizer in individual dishes garnished with a fresh sprig of mint and a cherry.

The core and peel from the pineapple may be kept and simmered with sugar and water for about ¾ hour, then the liquid strained off and put in the refrigerator for drinks.

OREGANO

A herb, highly regarded in Mediterranean cooking and one that is generally popular at the present time, is oregano (*Origanum vulgare*). It is one of the marjorams, the leaves being far more pungent and hot than the sweet marjoram and therefore used more sparingly. In most cases the plant or seed has been brought into this country by New Australians from their native hillsides, the species differing slightly in some provinces. This is perhaps the reason for some confusion over the name.

The scent varies also, according to soil and climate. It has some resemblance to marjoram, the leaves being smaller and rougher; it has a creeping root system and a rather sprawling habit. Oregano likes to grow in light, well-drained soil in a sunny position. Seed may be sown in the spring, or the roots may be divided in the autumn, winter or spring.

The name *Origanum* comes from Greek words meaning "joy of the mountains", which is very suitable because it grows in such a lively way, the bees clustering round the small white flowers when they appear, and the leaves seeming to absorb every ray of sunshine and clean, fresh air. Oregano is one of the most widely known herbs and is an ingredient of many classic national dishes. It is always included in Italian spaghetti dishes and in pizzas, in Chile con Carne from Mexico, and in numerous Spanish sauces (often under the name of wild marjoram). It is also used in guacamole, in tomato cookery, with mushroom dishes, with meat (especially veal and beef), and in a cream sauce to be poured over boiled white onions.

A plant, cherished carefully, will multiply to grand proportions. It is not wise to nibble oregano leaves indiscriminately for the powerful flavour is quite astonishing; the scent of oregano is warm, and provokes an image of the hearty food so full of flavour that it is used in, or accompanies.

Here are some suggestions for the use of the herb.

1. Oregano should be dried when in flower for the full benefit of the aroma; stalks may be picked as they flower, hung up to dry, and then used.

2. For a tasty grilled steak, rub it first with a cut clove of garlic, and then brush melted butter on to the steak with a dried branch of oregano. Some of the leaves and tiny flowers adhere to the meat. Grill, then turn the steak and repeat the process.

3. Rub dried oregano leaves, or put them freshly chopped, on top of tomatoes when baking, grilling or frying them.

4. Serve boiled spaghetti with a sauce mixed into it made from thinly sliced cloves of garlic, fried in oil until soft, peeled tomatoes, and oregano to taste. Top with grated Parmesan cheese.

STEAK KEBABS

Allowing ½ lb. meat for each person, cut fairly thick grilling steak into bite-sized cubes. Put the cubes onto skewers alternately with pieces of tomato, bacon, pineapple and pickled onions. Season with salt, pepper and dried oregano. Grill. These kebabs are ideal for a barbecue meal, and may be eaten with crisp bread rolls or a long French loaf, garlic flavoured.

PIZZA PIE

When preparing pizza pie it is worth the trouble to

make the bread dough with yeast in the traditional way for a dish loses its personality if made with "short cuts". The rich smell of the yeast, the smooth, elastic softness of the dough beneath the fingers, and the watching of it rise in a warm place all give such satisfaction that if only there were more time, making one's own bread would be a pleasurable and not difficult house-wifely task. Once there was enough dough left over from the pie to make a miniature loaf for the youngest member of the family—a wonderfully risen round loaf with a beige top which looked exactly like the illustrations in children's storybooks!

Bread Dough

¼ lb. plain flour	¼ oz. yeast
⅛ pint warm milk and water mixed	¼ teaspoon salt

Filling

4 peeled and cut tomatoes	1 dessertspoon fresh finely chopped oregano
1 tin anchovy fillets	
4 ozs thinly sliced cheese	Pepper and olive oil

Sift the flour and salt into a warm basin. Make a well in the centre and pour in the yeast which has been dissolved in a little of the warm milk and water. Fold the flour over the yeast with the fingers and keep folding it over until blended. Sprinkle a little flour over and round the dough, put a small blanket over the basin and leave in a warm place for the dough to rise (about 2 hours). The temperature should not be too hot or it will kill the yeast—85 degrees is a good temperature and this may be achieved with a gas or electric oven with careful watching. (A wood or coke stove is ideal for the making of bread dough of course, for the basin may be left where the warmth will reach it.) When ready take the warm basin and stand it for a few minutes where the dough will be kneaded to avoid any sharp drop in temperature. Take out the dough, sprinkle a little flour on the table and knead gently with the fingers until it reaches the right consistency. This is felt immediately by a subtle change in the dough—it becomes light and elastic. Roll it out very thinly in two discs, place one on the bottom of a lightly oiled oven-proof dish, spread with the tomatoes, season with pepper, lay the anchovies on the tomatoes, then the cheese and sprinkle the oregano on top. Pour 1 dessert-spoon of oil over all and then place the other disc on top just sealing the edges of the pie together with the fingers. Put in a hot oven (450 deg. electric) for 20 minutes and eat it warm. It makes an excellent luncheon dish accompanied with a French salad in the winter for four people.

SPAGHETTI BOLOGNESE

This method of serving Spaghetti Bolognese is rather different, and very tasty.

1 *lb. minced steak*
2 *oz. shortening*
1 *clove of garlic, finely chopped*
1 *onion, peeled and chopped*
½ *pint tomato puree or 1 lb. fresh, peeled tomatoes*
1 *cup stock (may be made with a beef cube)*
Salt and pepper
2 *teaspoons oregano*
½ *lb. spaghetti*

Garnish

1 *tomato, sliced*
1 *capsicum, sliced*
1 *cup finely grated cheese*
2 *rashers rindless bacon*
2 *teaspoons dried parsley*

Heat the shortening in a heavy saucepan, and fry the meat, garlic, and onion until brown. Add the tomato puree or the fresh tomatoes, and the stock, salt, pepper, and oregano. Cover, and simmer gently for 30 minutes.

In the meantime cook the spaghetti in plenty of boiling, salted water until it is soft (about 20 minutes), moving it occasionally with a fork so that the strands do not stick. Place it in a colander to drain, then pour hot water through it.

77

Take a greased casserole dish, put a layer of meat and sauce in the bottom, then half the spaghetti, another layer of meat and sauce, and finish with the rest of the spaghetti. To garnish, place the sliced tomato and capsicum over the top, sprinkle with the cheese, then the bacon (which has been cut into several pieces, each piece rolled up neatly and secured with a toothpick). Bake in a moderate oven (350°F.) until the cheese and bacon are cooked. Sprinkle the parsley over the top and bring the dish to the table.

OLIVES OREGANO

When black or green olives are steeped in a marinade of oil, herbs, and spices they acquire an added flavour and a mellow smoothness. Drain the olives for a short time before using them.

Prick 1 lb. olives with a silver fork and put them in a screw-top jar, add 1 cup vegetable oil, ½ teaspoon thyme, 1 teaspoon crushed peppercorns, and 2 teaspoons oregano. Top up with oil if necessary, cover, shake well and put into the refrigerator. Leave for at least 2 days, and use as required. Spear on wooden picks, or stone the olives and serve on vine leaves for lunch with black bread, two or three cheeses, and a light red wine. Especially delicious if eaten out of doors in the sunshine.

QUICHE LORRAINE

Line a buttered pie-dish with short-crust pastry (page 17). Prick all over. Remove the rind from ½ lb. bacon, cut into squares, and fry or grill until crisp. Place 3 or 4 whole thin slices of Cheddar cheese (obtainable in packets containing about 8 slices) on the pastry, then half the bacon and 1 teaspoon oregano. Repeat once more. Make a rich custard with ½ pint cream and 2 eggs, season with salt and pepper, and pour it over the cheese. Bake in a moderate oven (375°F.) for 30 minutes or until cooked. When cool, strew the top with stoned black olives.

PARSLEY

A bed of parsley is almost indispensable, and it is looked on in much the same way as mint—a herb that we take for granted. There are many varieties of parsley, the best known being curled parsley (*Petroselinum crispum*), fern-leaved parsley (*P. crispum filicinum*), and Italian parsley (*P. crispum neapolitanum*). An old saying that parsley seed goes six times to the Devil and back before germinating reveals how slow it is in this respect! When preparing to put in the seeds in the spring or autumn they may be soaked in water for twelve hours before planting to hasten germination.

Parsley is a biennial, although it may be kept as a perennial by cutting the flower stalks when they appear. If it is in the right position, moist and sheltered with some sun during the day, and in fairly rich soil, some of the plants could be allowed to go to seed, when they will self-sow with no trouble. To make the most of your plants, always pick from the outside, allowing the new leaves to develop from the middle. As it is not very interesting when dried, we are fortunate in this country to be able to grow parsley and eat it fresh all the year round.

Parsley has been a valued medicinal herb extolled by writers since ancient times. Culpeper, quite a latter-day enthusiast comparatively, lists several different varieties, and has written nearly three pages on its virtues in treating all manner of diseases, particularly kidney and liver complaints. He also says it is a good salad herb.

There are many traditions associated with this herb, one being that if parsley is planted around the onion bed it will keep away the onion fly; another that if parsley is thrown into a fish pond, it will cure sick fish. There is probably a lot of truth in many of these old beliefs.

Today, as a culinary herb, parsley fulfils many requirements. It is excellent for garnishing, and adding, in a chopped-up form, to white sauce, scrambled egg and mashed potatoes. Many people do not know how rich in vitamins it is. When green vegetables are scarce, a tablespoonful of chopped parsley on each plate will help to make up the deficiency. Fried parsley with fish is really delicious. Parsley jelly and parsley ice are two excellent ways of using this herb. There is also that delicacy made with parsley which should accompany most grills—Green Butter.

When people are unable to grow parsley because of climatic conditions or lack of garden space, it is sadly missed, but dried parsley is an excellent substitute. If it is dried quickly and carefully its colour and flavour in the food are indistinguishable from that of fresh parsley. So when your parsley grows in abundance, dry some of it— it will come in useful when this flavouring is wanted in a hurry, or when the garden yield is small. To dry it, spread sprigs on racks, or hang them in bunches in a warm, airy room. Parsley may also be dried quickly in a warm (*not* hot) oven. When crisp, rub through a sieve and seal in airtight containers. Use it for sprinkling on top of soups, for putting in mashed potato, all egg dishes, and in dumplings for a casserole or stew. Use it in sauces, mayonnaise and for parsley butter. Cut a lemon into wedges and dip the tops in dried parsley for an appetising garnish.

1 lb. noodles, any shape
½ teacup oil
2 tomatoes, peeled and
  chopped
3 cloves of garlic, finely
  cut up
2 tablespoons chopped
  capsicum

1 onion, chopped
1 lb. mushrooms, peeled
  and sliced
½ lb. bacon, grilled or fried,
  and cut into pieces
1 dessertspoon dried parsley
Salt and pepper
Grated Parmesan cheese

Heat the oil in a heavy saucepan and add the tomato, onion, garlic, capsicum, and mushrooms. Cook gently for 10 to 15 minutes, then add the bacon and parsley, with salt and pepper to taste. While preparing the mushroom mixture, have the noodles cooking in a quantity of boiling salted water, stirring them occasionally to prevent sticking. When soft, drain them well. Put into a warmed dish, cover with the hot mushroom mixture, and sprinkle generously with grated Parmesan cheese.

PARSLEY BUTTER

For grills, fish, and baked-jacket potatoes. Other herb butters may be made in the same way.

Soften ¼ lb. butter with a fork and work into it a few drops of lemon juice and 2 teaspoons dried parsley. Spread on a saucer and place in the refrigerator to harden. Cut into cubes and put them on a dish to be handed round at the table, or place cubes on the food just before serving it.

LAMB HARICOT

Have a leg of lamb cut right through into circles by the butcher. The meat is trimmed of fat and put into a large casserole with chopped onions, garlic, and tomatoes, a seasoning of salt, a few peppercorns, and a little stock. Bake with the lid on in a slow oven (250° to 300°F.) for 3 hours. Twenty minutes before serving, add 2 cups of cooked haricot beans. Finally, strew dried parsley liberally over it.

PARSLEY JELLY

Wash a big bunch of parsley (about 50 stalks). Put in a saucepan with enough water to cover, add the peel from a lemon and boil for about 1 hour. Strain the liquid into a basin and add the juice of 3 lemons. Measure, allowing a cup of sugar to every cup of liquid. Boil again until it begins to set. Drop in a little green colouring to improve the appearance. Put in jars, seal down and keep in a cool larder or refrigerator and eat it with chicken or fish.

FRIED PARSLEY

It is better not to wash the parsley, but if you do make sure it is absolutely dry before using. Break it up into sprigs and melt some butter in a frying pan. When the butter is hot and sizzling, but not black, put the sprigs in and let them fry quickly and crisply for about ½ minute or a little longer. Serve at once. The parsley should still be green, and not brown. Simple as this may sound, it takes a little practice which is well worth while.

PARSLEY ICE

1 *lemon*
½ *pint water*
½ *cup sugar*
1 *stiffly beaten egg white*

2 *tablespoons finely chopped parsley*
1 *tablespoon dry sherry and green colouring*

A water-ice is sometimes eaten with the meat course. In hot weather it is particularly refreshing. Put the juice and finely grated rind of the lemon in a saucepan with the sugar and water. Bring to the boil and stir in the parsley. Simmer for 5 minutes. Cool, add the sherry and green colouring. Put in an ice tray and freeze. When forming crystals take out and mix into the beaten egg white. Return to the refrigerator to harden. It looks tempting when turned out onto a dish embedded in ice.

ROSEMARY

This Mediterranean evergreen herb has mist-blue flowers that are loved by the bees. Rosemary was highly esteemed by the ancient Greeks and Romans, who introduced it to other countries. It was known to the Saxons and is referred to in one of the earliest herbals, the Saxon "Leech Book of Bald". It achieved great popularity in Tudor England for culinary, medicinal, and decorative reasons, and in those days was used for topiary work and was espaliered against walls. Shakespeare, Spenser, and many other poets have written about it. The wood of rosemary was used to make lutes and carpenter's rules.

There are several types: a rare gilded-leaved plant; a double-flowering kind; another with white flowers; one with broad leaves; a rosemary with horizontal branches which is valuable for rockery work; and the well-known bushy, upright rosemary which is the type most frequently used for seasoning. With the attractive symmetry of its narrow leaves and its rather stiff growing habit, this type makes a decorative hedge of medium height.

There is a great deal of herb lore surrounding rosemary: the French believed that the flowers rekindled lost energy, and they sometimes burnt branches of the bush for incense. It was also supposed to ward off black magic; it figured prominently on gay occasions such as weddings and banquets; and sprigs of rosemary to this day symbolize remembrance and friendship.

There should be a sunny nook in every garden for a rosemary bush. Starred with pale blue flowers nearly all the year round and with its narrow leaves green on one side and grey underneath, it is most attractive. The whole plant, especially the seeds, contains natural oils. This makes it valuable to use in the making of pot-pourri, hair rinses, toilet waters and scented rubbing lotions. Candied rosemary flowers, rosemary wine, rosemary honey and rosemary snow were once favoured confections. Today we know of it as a popular herb in Italian cooking, and the leaves used sparingly are excellent in certain food.

When we come upon a rosemary bush in the garden we may pause for a moment and remember some of the beautiful stories connected with it, and tell them to our children. It is not hard to imagine that fairies are supposed to use the flowers as their cradles.

There is the holy legend that during the flight into Egypt, the Virgin Mary threw her robe over a rosemary bush while she rested beside it. For ever afterwards the flowers which were previously white turred blue.

A picture called "The Legend of Rosemary", by Margaret W. Tarrant, shows Christ sitting on the ground while His Mother spreads His garments to dry on a rosemary bush. It is said this is the reason why the plant is so fragrant and "That bush forthgives, the faint, rare, sacred sweet of Him". (John Oxenham)

These, and other sacred legends were probably the reasons why it was believed that carrying a sprig of rosemary was proof against all evil and that it should be carried by brides, as well as decorating churches with it on festive occasions.

Rosemary will grow from seed, but it is quicker and easier to propagate from semi-hardwood cuttings, taken with a heel if possible, at any time of the year—February and March being the best months. It will flourish in a well-drained sunny position, sheltered from prevailing winds. Do not prune heavily, but if you are using and cutting it quite frequently once it is an established bush, this is all it needs.

The bracing and tonic effect of the leaves has always been valued. In *A Garden of Herbs* Eleanour Sinclair Rohde quotes from an old herbal: "Also if thou be feeble boyle the leaves in cleane water and washe thyself and thou shalt wax shiny." Among its many other virtues, rosemary stimulates the scalp and helps to relieve nervous headaches.

The name rosemary means "dew of the sea", and although the plant is hardy and will grow practically any-where—except through the severest winters, when it should be brought indoors—it flourishes best and has more flavour when grown near the sea.

When dried, the leaves become crisp and brittle, and are easily crumbled or chopped. The pungent scent of rosemary enhances certain food, particularly lamb, veal, pork, and beef. When added to a scone mixture it gives the scones a delicious flavour; it may often be used instead of thyme, and is excellent in pea soup, minestrone, spinach soup, and in casseroles and stews, or added to the water for boiling pickled pork.

BUTTERED CABBAGE SPINES AND ROSEMARY

A new and delicious vegetable was introduced to us by my aunt and uncle when they were on a visit from England: in fact, two vegetables are made from one. The pale-green "spines" are cut from the leaves of a cabbage with a pair of sharp kitchen scissors, giving a mound of crisp stalks and an-other of soft leaves with no stalks. Wrap these leaves in foil and put in the refrigerator for another occasion (when they may be shredded finely and steamed for a few minutes with a knob of butter). Put the cabbage spines or stalks into a saucepan with water and a little salt, bring to the boil, and simmer until they are tender (this may take from 20 to 30 minutes). Drain the stalks and pour over them a mixture of melted butter and 2 teaspoons of finely chopped or crumbled rosemary.

BEEF AND TOMATOES

In this hearty dish from the Mediterranean, the juices from the meat and vegetables mingle with the herbs and wine to form a savoury and aromatic sauce.

1½ *lb. shin of beef, roughly cut up*
3 *rashers of bacon, cut in squares*
1 *glass white or red wine*
4 *tomatoes, peeled*
2 *cloves of garlic, sliced*

2 *onions, peeled and sliced*
1 *dessertspoon chopped rosemary*
1 *bay leaf*
10 *juniper berries, crushed*
Salt and pepper

Put the meat into a casserole and cover it with the squares of bacon, then add the remaining ingredients. Bake with the lid on in a slow oven (250° to 300°F.) for 3 to 4 hours.

ROSEMARY SCONES

I have often served these scones to people who are interested in the unique flavour that herbs give to everyday food. As there could be nothing more everyday than scones, and as the recipe has been so popular, here it is.

2 *cups self-raising flour*
A pinch each of salt and sugar
1 *tablespoon butter*

1 *tablespoon finely chopped rosemary*
¾ *cup milk*

Sift the flour with salt and sugar, rub in the butter, add the rosemary, then the milk. Mix to a soft dough, roll lightly, and cut into squares. Place the squares close together on a greased and floured baking sheet, and bake in a hot oven (425°F.) for about 15 minutes.

Dried rosemary may be moistened first before chopping it; or crumble it between the fingers.

ROSEMARY SNOW

One of the prettiest conceits from sophisticated Tudor days was Rosemary Snow. Imagine the gorgeously apparelled people helping themselves to this confection in much the same way as we each dip our toast into the Cheese Fondue today.

(In *A Garden of Herbs*, by E. S. Rohde, from *A Book of Fruits and Flowers, 1653.*)

Take a quart of thick Creame, and five or six whites of Eggs, a saucer full of Sugar finely beaten and as much Rosewater, beat them all together and always as it riseth take it out with a spoon, then take a loaf of Bread, cut away the crust, set it in a platter, and a great Rosemary bush in the middest of it, then lay your Snow with a Spoon upon the Rosemary, and so serve it.

ROSEMARY HAIR RINSE

Pick a bunch of rosemary, cover it well with water and simmer it for ½ hour or more. A delicate fragrance and a tonic effect is given to the hair when given a final rinse with this preparation.

ROSES

When talking of herbs and their uses, roses must not be overlooked. Roses were once of supreme importance in a garden; not only were they admired for their beauty, but they were considered so useful that instead of allowing them to fall or wither away, they were collected and used in many ways. There are countless old recipes involving roses: rose syrup and rose vinegar, oil of roses, rose water, rose-scented snuff, candied rose petals, rosehip syrup, rose honey, rose "cakes", sweet sachets, potpourri and rose-petal jam and jelly.

Roses have been loved by the human race for centuries, and the most scented of all, the damask rose, was said to have been brought from Damascus by the Crusaders. We still love roses for their beauty and fragrance, and new varieties are grown every year, but whatever one's personal choice may be, they are essential in a garden. When cut and brought indoors they are always enchanting, whether carefully arranged in fine china, or massed together in a cottage jug.

Immortal poems have been written about the rose. They have been exquisitely painted on canvas, parchment and old china, and deft fingers have woven them into emblems, and embroidered them on tapestries.

Redouté, a French artist of a century ago, made a complete study of them and painted very many varieties in loving detail. Excellent prints of them are available.

The eglantine of Chaucer and Shakespeare is the sweet

briar rose, and it is the name Chaucer gives to his Prioress in *The Canterbury Tales*:

> *There was also a nun, a Prioress*
> *Whose smile was simple, quiet, even coy.*
> *The only oath she swore was, "By Saint Loy!"*
> *And she was known as Sister Eglantine.*

Constance Spry in her *Constance Spry Cookery Book* gives many recipes for using roses in cooking. She suggests that a spoonful or two of rose jam or jelly added to certain sweets and ices gives them a delicious perfume and flavour.

ROSE PETAL JAM
(From *Herbs and Herb Gardening*, by Eleanour Sinclair Rohde.)

It is essential to use red, fragrant Roses. To fifty fully opened Roses allow two pints of water, preferably clean rainwater or distilled water and 3 lb. of the best preserving sugar. Boil the sugar and water till it candies a little. Add the juice of a small Lemon and the Rose petals. Stir well and bring to the boil. Put in a pat of butter to clear the scum and then simmer for quite an hour. It is necessary to stir very frequently, every five minutes or so, or the colour will be brown instead of red. Pour into pots and cover when cold.

I have made this recipe using ordinary tap water, and it really makes quite a large quantity.

ROSE VINEGAR

Fill a glass or crockery vessel with petals from scented roses and pour 1 pint of white vinegar over them. Cover and allow to infuse for 2 weeks, preferably in the sun. Strain, and use in the same way as tarragon vinegar.

GREEN SALAD WITH ROSE PETALS

When ready to serve a lettuce salad, toss with a French dressing made with rose petal vinegar, add 1 tablespoon of rose petals from the tiny roses (or the smallest petals from scented roses) and mix again. Excellent for a luncheon with cold poultry.

CANDIED ROSE PETALS

Make sure the rose petals are not bruised and are thoroughly dry. Coat each one carefully with beaten white of egg applied with a small clean paint brush. Dust with castor sugar. Turn them over and repeat the process. Dry in the sun, occasionally turning them. When they are quite dry store in airtight jars between layers of grease-proof paper.

I can remember only pink ones being used; they were delicious on trifles with sugared violets and silver cashews nestling on whipped cream. They may also be used for decorating cakes.

HONEY OF ROSES

(In *A Garden of Herbs*, by E. S. Rohde, and from an old recipe by T. Tryon in *A Treatise of Cleanness in Meates, 1692*.)

Cut the white heels from Red Roses, take half a pound of them and put them into a stone jar, and pour on them three pints of boiling water. Stir well and let them stand twelve hours. Then press off the liquor, and when it has settled add to it five pounds of honey. Boil it well, and when it is of the consistence of a thick syrup it is ready to put away.

POT-POURRI

To about 40 roses allow the following spices and oils:

½ oz. oil of geranium	1 oz. ground nutmeg
½ oz. oil of lavender	1 oz. coriander seed
2 or 3 cinnamon sticks	4 oz. orris root powder
1 oz. whole cloves	About 4 oz. common salt

Gather the roses on a dry day after the dew has left them. Spread them out in a cool, airy place, turning them frequently. When the petals are paper dry put them with the salt into a crockery or glass vessel with an airtight lid. To each handful of petals allow a smaller one of salt.

Cover and leave, stirring twice a day for 5 days. In the meantime gather all the scented leaves and flowers that are suitable, about a handful of each according to what is available and personal taste. Scented geranium leaves, particularly the rose-scented, are excellent, as well as lavender flowers, rosemary flowers, carnations, bay leaves, lemon-scented verbena, balm, jasmine, eau-de-Cologne mint, orange blossoms, violets and wallflowers.

These should be drying on sieves or on sheets of paper. On the fifth day add these ingredients to the roses and salt.

Put some of the orris powder in a cup and add the oils, stirring well until the consistency is no longer moist but powdery. A chemist advised me to do this, as the powder quickly "takes up" the valuable oil which is then added to the pot-pourri with the rest of the orris powder and spices, and is evenly distributed. Dried sliced angelica root and a little orange and lemon peel, with no pith adhering to the skin, may be added too.

Stir all the ingredients very well, cover and leave for 3 or 4 weeks. It may be stirred occasionally, in fact it is a pleasure to do so.

If the pot-pourri becomes too dry add more salt, and if too moist add more orris root powder.

As the spices retain their strength for years, dried flowers may be added from time to time. Rosemary and lavender flowers are especially good as they contain essential aromatic oils. When put into suitable bowls this makes a very delightful gift.

ROSE WATER

Nicholas Culpeper the seventeenth century herbalist says of rose water in *Culpeper's Complete Herbal*: "Red rose water is well known, and of a similar use on all occasions, and better than the damask rose-water, it is cooling, cordial, refreshing, quickening the weak and faint spirits, used either in meats or broths, to wash the temples, to smell at the nose, or to smell the sweet vapours out of a perfume pot, or cast into a hot fire-shovel."

There are many recipes for making rose water, but most of them are tedious and difficult with their instructions for distilling. The following recipe is quite simple. Some people use it in finger bowls, or put a little of it in a basin of water for guests to wash their hands.

Take 2 handfuls of scented red rose petals and put them in a jug or earthen pot. Pour over them 2 pints of water and ½ lb. sugar. Let them steep for 1 hour. Take the water and roses and pour from one vessel into another until the water is scented with the flowers. Strain and keep in a cool place.

SAGE

Sage (*Salvia officinalis*) is a popular perennial herb grown by many people today. It is one of the old favourites that has not been lost to us, probably because, for centuries, it was highly esteemed for its health-giving properties. "Why should a man die who has sage in his garden?" is an old proverb.

Sage prefers a light soil and a sunny position. When it has finished blooming cut off the flower stalks, and it will soon grow into a compact bush between two and three feet high. Eventually it is wise to put in new plants, and this is easily done by breaking roots off from the old bush, or by sowing the seed when it is ripe.

According to the old writers, sage leaves are at their most beneficial in the spring, before the flower stalks begin to lengthen. It is also the best time for drying this herb.

The leaves are very pungent and slightly acrid, but they have a very pleasant flavour when cooked. Sage and onion stuffing with duck is well known, and leek tart flavoured with sage is delicious.

Halved, buttered tomatoes piled with small mounds of scented, dried sage, and baked until tender, go well with grilled pork chops and apple sauce.

A sage-cheese spread is simply made by beating 3 teaspoons of dried sage and a few drops of lemon juice into 4 oz. cream cheese.

Rub a joint of meat with dried sage before roasting it.

Try sage as a seasoning for meat rissoles, meat loaf, cheese dishes, eggs and fish.

The leek (*Allium porrum*) is the emblem of Wales. It is also a "pot herb". Early plant lists indicate that "herbs for the pot" were the forerunners of many present day vegetables.

Leek pie with yeast pastry is an old favourite. The following recipe, Leek Tart with Sage, is delicious and simple to make. It has a very delicate flavour and is more palatable to those who find onions too strong. It goes very well with cold meat (lamb or mutton particularly) served with red currant jelly, or a sharp apple jelly. It is also excellent on its own with a French salad, and may be eaten either hot or cold. When preparing leeks for cooking, cut off the roots and leaves, leaving about one inch of the green, and wash very well.

LEEK TART WITH SAGE

1 *doz. leeks*	1 *tablespoon finely*
½ *cup cream or top of milk*	*chopped sage leaves*
1 *egg*	2 *or* 3 *rashers of bacon*
1 *tablespoon chopped*	*Salt and pepper*
parsley	*Short pastry*

Cut the leeks into thin circles, put them in a saucepan with a little water and simmer gently until soft. Drain, and add the chopped herbs, the beaten egg and the cream, mixing it all together. Adjust seasoning.

Line a lightly floured pie dish with thinly rolled short pastry. Prick it well, and spoon in the leek mixture. Cut the bacon into small squares (after removing the rind) and arrange on top of the tart. Bake in a medium to hot oven for about 20 minutes.

The short pastry I make is a recipe from my husband's family, and known as Emily's Pastry. Hers was so light that it almost blew away, and yet it was rich and full of flavour.

EMILY'S PASTRY

1 *good cup S.R. flour*
2 *oz. butter*
½ *cup cold water with a little lemon juice added*

Pinch salt (and a pinch of sugar when using for sweets)

Sift dry ingredients. Rub butter and flour together with finger-tips. Add water gradually and mix lightly with knife. Roll lightly. Place in a fairly hot oven for 20 minutes. Do not brown too quickly. Always open and close oven door very gently—*never bang.*

Cheese flavoured with sage has been favoured by country people for years. Welsh rarebit made with beer and flavoured with sage makes a particularly appetizing Sunday night meal.

WELSH RAREBIT WITH SAGE

½ *lb. grated tasty cheese*
1 *dessertspoon finely chopped sage leaves*

1 *cup beer*
Salt, pepper, ½ teaspoon mustard

Warm the beer in a saucepan, and gradually add the cheese, then the sage, salt, pepper and mustard. Stir well until the cheese has melted. Serve hot with triangles of hot buttered toast.

SAGE AND ONION STUFFING

(From Mrs Beeton's *Poultry and Game.*)

Take 4 large onions, 10 sage leaves, ¼ of a lb. of bread-crumbs, 1½ oz. of butter, salt and pepper to taste, and 1 egg.

Peel the onions, put them into boiling water, let them simmer for 5 minutes or rather longer, and, just before they are taken out, put in the sage leaves for a minute or two to take off their rawness. Chop both these very fine, add the bread, seasoning, and butter, and work the whole together with the yolk of an egg, when the stuffing will be ready for use. It should be rather highly seasoned, and the sage leaves should be very finely chopped. Many cooks do not parboil the onions in the manner just stated, but merely use them raw, but the stuffing then is not nearly so mild, and, to many tastes, its strong flavour would be very objectionable. When made for goose, a portion of the liver of the bird, simmered for a few minutes and very finely minced, is frequently added to this stuffing; and where economy is studied, the egg and butter may be omitted.

This should be sufficient for 1 goose, or a pair of ducks.

ISABELLE'S SAGE AND CHEESE OMELET

1 *cup grated Cheddar*
cheese
1 *cup milk*
2 *eggs, separated*
1 *cup soft breadcrumbs*

1 *dessertspoon grated*
onion
2 *teaspoons chopped sage*
Salt and pepper

This is an excellent luncheon or supper dish.

Warm the milk, and add it to the beaten egg yolks and other ingredients (except the egg whites). Add salt and pepper. Allow the mixture to stand for 1 hour. Fold in the whipped egg whites. Bake in a buttered dish in a fairly moderate oven (350°F.) for 30 minutes.

SAGE BREAD

This sage-flavoured bread is well worth the small amount of time and effort spent in preparing it. As it is a particularly quick method, it could become a winter standby to accompany roast meat, casseroles, and thick stews, or for Sunday night supper with bowls of hot soup. It is delicious with Camembert and coffee.

½ *oz. dry yeast*
3 *tablespoons warm water*
1 *lb. plain flour*
1 *teaspoon salt*
2 *dessertspoons dried sage*
1 *teaspoon allspice*

1 *teaspoon celery seed*
1 *dessertspoon sugar*
1 *scant cup warm milk*
1 *oz. butter*
1 *lightly beaten egg*

Dissolve the yeast in the warm water. Sift the flour and salt into a bowl, and mix in the sage, allspice, celery seed, and sugar. Form a well in the centre and pour into it the warm (not hot) milk in which the butter has been melted, then the egg and the dissolved yeast. Mix lightly, turn out onto a

95

floured surface, and knead. Put into a greased bowl, cover
with a small blanket, and leave in a warm place to rise for
1 hour. Turn out onto a floured surface once more. (In cold
weather, first stand the warmed bowl on the table for a few
minutes so that there is not too great a drop in temperature
for the dough when it is turned out onto the board.) Knead
and shape into a cottage loaf or two small loaves, place on a
greased baking sheet, and allow to stand for 15 minutes. Bake
in a hot oven (425°F.) for about 30 minutes. If the top is
browning too much, cover with a sheet of tinfoil and reduce
oven temperature by 50 degrees.

SAGE HAIR TONIC

Here is an old "receipt" from *Lotions and Potions*, a collection of their ancestors' recipes compiled by members of the
Women's Institute, England:

Take 1 tablespoonful each of tea and of dried sage. Put into
a 2-lb. jam jar, cover with boiling water, and simmer for
2 hours. Cool and strain. Rub into the scalp four or five times
a week. Gradually greyness will disappear, and hair becomes
dark brown. Will keep for a week; add 1 tablespoonful of
rum, gin, or eau-de-Cologne for longer keeping.

TO WHITEN THE TEETH

Rub with sage leaves. This hint also came from *Lotions
and Potions*.

SAGE TEA

If you have sage and lemon balm growing, here is a whole-
some old beverage quoted in *A Garden of Herbs* by Eleanour
Sinclair Rohde from *The New Art of Cookery*, by Richard
Briggs (many years Cook at the Globe Tavern, Fleet Street,
The White Hart Tavern, Holborn, and at the Temple Coffee
House, 1788): "Take a little sage, a little Balm, put it into a
pan, slice a Lemon, peel and all, a few knobs of sugar, one
glass of white wine; pour on these two or three quarts of
boiling water; cover it, and drink when thirsty. When you
think it strong enough of the herbs take them out otherwise
it will make it bitter."

SAVORY

Summer Savory (*Satureia hortensis*) and winter savory (*S. montana*) are the two popular varieties of this genus for use in cooking. Seed of the summer savory, which is an annual, is sown in the spring, the plant growing to about one-and-a-half feet high. Winter savory, a perennial, may be grown from seed also, but it is usually more satisfactory to divide the roots in the spring, when it will grow rapidly into a bushy shrub a little over a foot high. A pleasing idea would be to plant a dwarf hedge of winter savory, as in Tudor days. It also makes an attractive plant for herbaceous borders. Grow both varieties of savory in light soil in the sun.

At first glance the savories resemble thyme; however, on closer inspection, you will see that the leaves are longer and quite narrow. Like thyme the leaves are pungent, but with a hot peppery flavour. It is said that rubbing a leaf on a bee sting will relieve the pain.

Savory retains its flavour well when dried, and is a most useful herb. Traditionally known as "the bean herb", it should accompany all bean dishes, just as mint goes with peas, and basil with tomatoes. Savory with chopped chives and parsley makes an excellent stuffing for duck. It is a pleasant accompaniment for lamb, pork, and veal, and gives a delightfully different flavour to tomato sauce.

Winter savory is a well-contented habitué of the window trough. Do not plant it, however, with parsley or chives as it may take over the whole container.

A mellow and fragrant jelly to eat with turkey, ham, and other meat dishes, equally delicious on buttered hot rolls and scones. The glowing colour reminds me of how the jelly described by Flora Thompson in *Lark Rise to Candleford* must have looked when ready to eat—jelly that was strained and sweetened and laced with port, sufficient to colour it a deep ruby, and cleared with eggshells, and strained again, then poured into a flannel jellybag and hung from a hook all night to let its contents ooze through, then poured into a mould and allowed yet one more night in which to set.

This recipe is delicious, and it is very easy to make.

1 *bottle dark grape juice*	4 *oz. powdered pectin*
2 *dessertspoons dried*	3 *cups sugar*
savory	*Juice of a lemon*

Heat the grape juice and savory together, then add the pectin and bring to the boil. Add the sugar and lemon juice and boil for 2 minutes, stirring all the time. Remove from the stove, skim, and seal into small jars immediately.

SAVORY TOMATO SAUCE

This is an excellent sauce with grills.

Peel and chop 1 lb. ripe tomatoes and simmer them in a saucepan with 1 finely chopped onion, 2 teaspoons dried savory, and 1 cup water, adding salt and pepper to taste. When cooked, rub through a sieve. Melt 2 oz. butter, blend in 1 heaped tablespoon plain flour, and gradually add the sauce. Stir until thickened. Bottle.

SAVORY STUFFED LEG OF LAMB

1 *small leg of lamb, boned*	6 *juniper berries, crushed*
1 *cup soft breadcrumbs*	*A few pieces of butter*
2 *teaspoons dried savory*	1 *cup red or white wine*
1 *dessertspoon chopped*	¼ *lb. butter or margarine,*
white onion	*melted*
1 *clove of garlic, finely*	*Salt and pepper*
chopped	

98

Mix together the breadcrumbs, savory, onion, garlic, crushed juniper berries, and the pieces of butter, adding salt and pepper to taste. Stuff the leg, fasten it with skewers, and put it into a baking dish with the wine and the melted butter. Bake in a moderate oven (350° to 375°F.) for 1 to 1½ hours, basting frequently. Add a little more wine if necessary. To serve, lift the leg onto a hot dish and pour pan juices over it. Surround with well-drained boiled potatoes coated with butter and chopped parsley.

SAVORY STUFFING FOR FISH

1 *cup soft breadcrumbs*	2 *oz. butter*
Grated rind and juice of	1 *tablespoon finely*
1 *lemon*	*chopped onion*
1 *dessertspoon finely*	1 *egg*
chopped savory	*Salt and pepper*

Soften the butter in a frying pan and gently fry the onion without browning. Add to the other ingredients in a bowl, binding the mixture with the egg. 1 doz. oysters, or 1 cup shelled prawns may be added with advantage to the stuffing.

FRIED TRIPE AND WINTER SAVORY

1½ *lb. tripe*	1 *tablespoon fresh or*
1 *chopped white onion*	1 *dessertspoon dried*
1½ *cups oil*	*savory*
2 *thinly sliced cloves of*	1 *tin or ½ lb. fresh*
garlic	*mushrooms*
	Flour

Simmer the tripe for about an hour. Drain in a colander, allowing the cold tap to run over it. Fry the onion and garlic in the oil until soft. Cut the tripe into cubes, roll in flour and add to the onion and garlic. Fry until golden, adding more oil if necessary. Put in a fireproof dish, add the mushrooms, savory and ½ pint of stock. Cover and simmer in a slow oven for 1 hour. Even people who don't care for tripe, usually like it this way.

2 lb. fish fillets

1 tablespoon finely
  chopped savory

2 peeled and cored apples
  cut into wedges

3 finely sliced shallots

1 breakfast cup cider

Soft breadcrumbs and
  butter

Roll the fillets in flour and put them in a buttered fire-proof dish with the apple, savory and shallots. Season with salt and freshly ground pepper. Pour the cider in slowly and carefully. Top with breadcrumbs which have been lightly fried in butter. Bake in a moderate oven for about 20 minutes. The fragrance of apple and cider united with spicy savory combines well with fish.

SCENTED~LEAVED GERANIUMS

Scented geraniums are a valuable addition to the herb garden, not only because their leaves impart subtle depths of perfume to pot-pourri, but also because they may be used to flavour certain foods. All geranium leaves have a rather pungent quality. This is much more marked in some kinds than in others, and there are a number of varieties whose leaves are redolent of familiar scents which brings to mind the interesting fact that plant scents have their own tones and variations, just as in music and colour.

There seems to be an essential element which makes some plants smell of apples, lemons, roses and so on. The apple-scented geranium, *Pelargonium odoratissimum*, for instance, smells strongly of Granny Smith apples even when lightly brushed in passing. It is a delicate spreading plant, with round, green leaves and fragile, white flowers, valuable for borders or in the rockery.

The nutmeg-scented geranium, *P. fragrans*, at first glance is rather similar, but it is of more upright growth, and when the ruffled leaves are crushed the spicy scent reminds one of freshly ground nutmegs. The rose-scented geranium, from which the well-known oil of geranium is extracted, is said to be *P. capitatum*, although there is another variety known as attar-of-roses, or *P. graveolens*, which is thought by many to be the rose geranium, its leaves having much the same elusive perfume. The variety Lady Plymouth is also rose scented, and the leaves are variegated green and gold.

The lemon-scented geranium, *P. limonium,* has leaves smelling of lemons and something more, which is probably verbena, and this may be the reason why it is often called "lemon-scented verbena". The crisp leaves are long, very serrated and decorative, and the flowers, a delicate shade of pinky-mauve, are small and single. One or two leaves are often used to flavour jellies, custards, rice puddings and sponge cakes; when dried they give their warm yet lemony fragrance to pot-pourri, and the dried flowers, too, impart their fragrance and colour. The leaves of this variety are excellent for use in flower arrangements.

Some other varieties smelling of lemons are *P. asperium,* which has similar leaves to the lemon-scented, except that they are very sticky. The decorative *P. crispum variegata* looks like a miniature cypress tree and the lemon-scented leaves are small, curly and variegated.

Many people consider that *P. tomentosum* is the most fascinating variety of the scented-leaved geraniums. The peppermint-scented leaves are large and velvety, of a clear-green colour, delightfully described by Gertrude Jekyll to be "thick as a fairy's blanket, soft as a vicuna robe". There are recipes for using the leaves to make peppermint jelly, and if you wish to follow a Greek custom flavour apple jelly by putting them, as well as other sweet-scented geranium leaves (only two or three at a time), into the preserving pan during the last five minutes of cooking.

Take them out before sealing the jelly in pots, but a fresh leaf may be put in for decoration and flavour. In flower arrangements the peppermint-scented leaves lend contrast in texture and form against other leaves and as a soft foil for flowers; red roses, nestling against the tender green of these leaves are particularly enchanting.

The plant itself is rampant and sprawling, and likes room to grow; the small white flowers, as is often the case with sweet-scented geraniums, are insignificant.

An interesting scented variety is the coconut-scented *P. enossularoides*, which has crimson flowers and leaves similar to the apple-scented geranium. Another is *P. abrotanifolium*, sometimes known as southernwood, the scent of the leaves being exactly like that of southern·wood or lad's love.

Clorinda is sweetly named and lovely to look at with eucalyptus-scented leaves of brightish-green and single pelargonium-like flowers of rich cyclamen. *P. denticulatum* has very cut and fragile leaves, which are sticky and smell warm and spicy. It has mauve flowers. Fair Helen or Fair Ellen is an old favourite with large, pungent oak leaves and magenta flowers. Besides the ones mentioned here there are many more, an almost bewildering variety, and all a lesson in scent perception.

Last but not least in this chapter of geraniums is the little herb Robert, or Geranium Robert, as it is sometimes called. It is an annual with a delicate trailing habit, small round leaves and single deep pink flowers; today it makes a delightful herbaceous plant, but it was once valued in herbal therapy for its styptic qualities.

All the scented-leaved geraniums may be dried and used in pot-pourri except the sticky varieties. It is important to dry the peppermint-scented leaves carefully as they are inclined to retain moisture and to mildew. Spread them out on paper in warm, dry weather when there is no humidity in the air. Constance Spry suggests that scented geranium leaves can improve the flavour of a cake.

4 *eggs*	*Rose-geranium leaves*
6 *oz. sugar*	1 *level tablespoon butter*
1¼ *cups S.R. flour*	4 *tablespoons hot water*
2 *level tablespoons cornflour*	*Pinch salt*

Separate the egg whites and beat until stiff, gradually add the sugar and beat until it is dissolved, then gently mix in the egg yolks. Sift the flour, cornflour and salt 3 times, lightly fold it into the cake mixture, have the butter melted and the hot water ready and fold in carefully. Grease and lightly flour two 8 in. cake tins, lay rose-geranium leaves on the bottom of the tins and pour in the cake mixture. Bake in a fairly hot oven (automatic electric 400°) on the bottom shelf for 20 minutes. Turn out on a wire tray and leave to cool. The geranium leaves may be left on the bottom of the cake until ready for filling, allowing the flavour to penetrate. Fill the sponge with cream and sift a little icing sugar on the top. The perfume from the geranium leaves will linger, giving the cake a subtle fragrance.

LEMON-SCENTED BAKED CUSTARD

3 *eggs*	1 *medium-sized lemon-scented geranium leaf*
1 *pint milk*	
2 *tablespoons sugar*	*A little butter*

Break the eggs into a fireproof dish, add the sugar and beat together with a fork. Pour the milk gradually on the eggs, beating all the time. Dot with butter and place the geranium leaf in the centre of the custard. Put the dish in a pan containing about an inch of cold water and cook in a medium oven until the custard is set, about ¾ hour. The geranium leaf gently imparts its lemony aroma to the custard —a plain rice pudding may be flavoured in the same way.

PEPPERMINT JELLY

4 *lemons*	*Green colouring or crème de menthe*
1 *cup sugar*	
1 *pint very hot water*	*Peppermint-scented geranium leaves*
3 *dessertspoons gelatine*	

Pick and wash a bunch of peppermint-scented geranium leaves, put them in a basin and bruise with a spoon. Squeeze the lemons and pour the juice on the geranium leaves, add the sugar. Cover the basin and leave for at least 2 hours. Strain the liquid through a sieve, pressing all moisture out of the leaves. Dissolve the gelatine in a little of the hot water, pour the rest of the water and dissolved gelatine into the peppermint-scented liquid. Add a tablespoon of crème de menthe if you wish, or a few drops of green colouring, and stir well. Pour the jelly into a dish and decorate the centre with a peppermint-scented geranium leaf, leave to set.

BAKED APPLES WITH GERANIUM LEAVES

4 green cooking apples
1 tablespoon apple jelly

4 apple-scented geranium leaves
A little butter

Wash the apples, cut a little of the peel away from the top and core (a clean wooden "dolly" clothes peg is most efficient). Put a little butter into the hollows in the apples, add 1 teaspoon of apple jelly to each apple and top with an apple-scented geranium leaf. Stand the apples in a little water in a fireproof dish and bake in a medium to hot oven until just soft. Pour the liquid from the dish into a saucepan, add 1 tablespoon of sugar and boil for a few minutes, add a little red colouring and pour the syrup over the apples. Eat them hot with thick cream, and the geranium leaves, which become crisp, are edible too.

TARRAGON

Tarragon (*Artemisia dracunculus*) is a herb renowned for its distinctive aromatic flavour. The most fragrant culinary variety, known as French, or "true" tarragon does not set seed, while the inferior Russian tarragon does. In this country there has been much controversy as to whether there is any true tarragon here at all.

The only way to have French tarragon in the garden is to plant a root of it, and even then, perhaps, connoisseurs, who have travelled widely, will be doubtful about whether it is the real thing. The climatic and soil conditions often affect the characteristic flavour of a plant to a greater or lesser degree. The dried leaves are more aromatic than the fresh, although a bite into the green tartness will show the flavour pungent enough. Grow the plant in light, rather poor soil in a warm position, allowing it to absorb as much sunlight as possible so that it will then have the opportunity of showing what may be achieved in the way of flavour.

Tarragon is the most palatable of the artemisias. It is tartly aromatic, and its uses in the kitchen are many. The leaves when steeped in white vinegar impart a fragrant bouquet. It is usual to add a little chopped tarragon to such sauces as Hollandaise, Béarnaise, and Tartare. Tarragon gives chicken stuffing a delightfully different flavour. It is excellent in fish and shellfish dishes, in veal and rabbit dishes, with chicken livers, and in chicken or fish soups. It may be added to sour cream sauces, mayonnaise, and French dressing. When using the dried herb, chop it finely and begin with 1 teaspoon unless otherwise stated in the recipe: a little more can then be added according to taste.

Tarragon vinegar is quickly made. Pack a glass jar with tarragon leaves, pour white vinegar over, cover and infuse for two weeks. Strain and pour into bottles. A fresh branch of tarragon put into the bottle not only adds strength to the vinegar, but looks effective.

Some of the Artemisia family, to which tarragon belongs, are not culinary herbs, but were once used in medicine, and in the household. They were grown in every cottage garden. It is not out of place therefore to mention them here. We know them by their homely old names of lad's love, dusty miller and old woman.

Southernwood (*A. abrotanum*), sometimes called old man or lad's love, is a three foot high ornamental shrub with the most delicate grey-green foliage. Bitter-sweet describes the scent and flavour of this herb. It is very aromatic with a slight touch of ether about it. Perhaps this is why it was once a remedy for insomnia!

Wormwood (*A. absinthum*) is also one of the bitter herbs, and is used in the making of absinthe. It was highly valued for its medicinal qualities and was also strewn amongst clothes to keep away moths. "It is a very noble bitter, and succeeds in procuring an appetite", observes Culpeper. It is said to be "Dian's bud" which Oberon used to waken Titania in *A Midsummer Night's Dream*.

Sea wormwood (*A. stelleriana*), or old woman, is yet another of this family, a much lower-growing variety and not so aromatic, and as its botanical name indicates, it likes sandy soil.

SAUCE TARTARE

1 egg yolk
½ cup olive oil
1 tablespoon tarragon
vinegar
1 teaspoon chopped
capers (optional)

1 dessertspoon chopped
olives
1 dessertspoon chopped
tarragon
A little mustard, salt and
pepper

Put the egg yolk into a basin with the mustard, salt and pepper. Drop the oil onto this gradually, stirring well all the time until the mixture is smooth and thick. Beat in the vinegar carefully and add the olives, tarragon and capers. Serve with Fish.

CHICKEN SUPREME WITH PEACHES

1 fowl
2 tablespoons butter
1½ tablespoons flour
1 egg
½ cup thick cream

4 ripe peaches
2 tablespoons finely
chopped tarragon
Salt and pepper

Put the fowl on a wire sieve in a large saucepan and steam it gently until it is tender. Lift out, cut into pieces and arrange on a large plate. Keep it warm. Melt the butter, add the flour, stirring until it is well blended. Gradually add ¾ pint of stock in which the chicken was cooked and stir until it thickens. Adjust seasoning. Beat the egg and cream together and pour into the sauce. Stir for ½ minute, remove from the stove, and mask the chicken with it. Peel and cut the peaches into halves, poach gently, drain and arrange around the chicken. Sprinkle with tarragon and serve very hot. If fresh peaches are not available, the best tinned peaches will do.

CRAB AND AVOCADO MOULD

2 cups crabmeat
2 avocados peeled and
diced
1 cup diced celery
1 tin tomato soup

1½ tablespoons gelatine
1 tablespoon chopped
tarragon
Salt and pepper

Mix the crabmeat, avocado, tarragon and celery together, adjust seasoning. Soak the gelatine in ½ cup of heated tomato soup for 5 minutes then stir it slowly into the remainder of the soup. Pour this over the crabmeat mixture and set it in a mould. When firm, turn it out on a bed of watercress or finely shredded lettuce surrounded by slices of lemon.

HOLLANDAISE SAUCE

Hollandaise and Béarnaise sauce are similar in composition. Other well-known sauces, such as Mousseline and Choron, are based on these two, the ingredients that make the variation being added at the end.

There are several methods of making Hollandaise, but I have found the following recipe the most satisfactory. It is important to have all ingredients to hand. If you haven't a double saucepan, a bowl stood in gently boiling water will do instead.

2 egg yolks	*¼ lb. butter*
1 tablespoon cream	*1 teaspoon chopped*
1 dessertspoon lemon juice	*tarragon*
1 tablespoon water	*Salt and pepper*

Into a small bowl within easy reach of the stove put the yolks, cream, lemon juice, and water, with salt and pepper to taste. When water is boiling gently in the bottom half of a double saucepan, melt the butter in the top half, then with a wire whisk beat in the contents of the small bowl. Continue beating until the mixture thickens, then remove immediately from the heat, beating a little longer to prevent curdling (if this happens, quickly beat in a few drops of cold water and another egg yolk). Add the tarragon.

Hollandaise sauce should be served lukewarm. It may be poured into the cavity of ripe, stoned avocado pears for an entrée. It is delicious with asparagus, young beans, grilled fish, and other finely textured food.

CHICKEN LIVERS IN WINE

1½ lb. chicken livers	*2 teaspoons chopped*
¼ lb. butter	*tarragon*
2 cloves of garlic, finely	*1 tablespoon plain flour*
chopped	*½ pint red or white wine*
1 teaspoon dried marjoram	*Salt and pepper*

Wash the chicken livers, cut in half, and simmer gently in the butter with the garlic until cooked. Add the tarragon, marjoram, and flour, season with salt and pepper, and turn the livers until the flour browns. Gradually add the wine, stirring until the gravy is smooth and thickened. Serve with boiled rice.

CHICKEN MIMOSA

Steam a chicken until the flesh is tender. Keep the chicken stock for making the sauce. Remove the flesh from the bones while the bird is still hot, and cut into thin slices. Make a stuffing by mixing together 2 cups soft breadcrumbs, 3 teaspoons seasoning herbs, 1 dessertspoon chopped tarragon, 1 dessertspoon chopped shallots, and a little grated lemon rind, adding salt and pepper to taste. Spread this mixture in the bottom of a buttered fireproof dish and lay the chicken slices on it.

Make Sauce Suprême by melting in a saucepan $\frac{1}{4}$ lb. butter, blending in $\frac{1}{2}$ cup plain flour, and gradually adding $1\frac{1}{2}$ pints chicken stock. Stir until thickened. Lightly beat together 5 eggs, $\frac{1}{4}$ pint cream, and a sprinkling of salt and pepper. Pour a little of the thickened chicken liquid from the saucepan onto these eggs, then add this to the contents of the saucepan. Allow to cook for a few minutes (do not boil), stirring all the time. Now pour the sauce over the chicken pieces in the fireproof dish. Bake in a slow oven (300°F.) for about 45 minutes, or until the sauce has set. Sprinkle the top with the sieved yolks of 2 hard-boiled eggs.

This dish may be made in advance and gently heated through in the oven before being served hot with French-style peas and Saffron Risotto. The fruity flavour of white burgundy is an ideal companion for this rich and savoury dish.

TARRAGON VINEGAR

If you have no fresh tarragon growing, steep 1 heaped tablespoon of dried tarragon leaves in 1 pint of white vinegar. Leave for at least 2 weeks before using. The tarragon need not be strained off.

THYME

As there are numerous varieties of thyme, it may become a fascinating hobby for the interested gardener to collect as many different kinds as possible, not only for the herb garden, but also for rockeries and to cover inhospitable ground.

Thyme is truly the enchanted herb. E. S. Rohde declares that "wild thyme has always been a favourite with fairies" and she goes on to give an old recipe "To enable one to see the Fairies". It is directed that the "vial glasse in which the liquid is made must first be washed with rose-water and marygolde water", and the flowers gathered towards the east from the side of a fairy throne. Indulgent fancy though it may be, it is the small, scented plants which creep so joyfully over the ground with their softly hued flowers, the graceful foxgloves and campanulas that rise in spires against a green garden, and the native *Grevillea rosmarinifolia* with its delicate rose and cream spider flowers, that entrance all who see them, and make us feel that perhaps in some gardens Ariel may be lurking and softly singing: "Where the bee sucks, there suck I."

Edna Walling delights us by writing: "Luxuries of luxuries! I've been lying on my own thyme lawn, there was just enough room to turn over without landing on to the surrounding rock plants. You haven't lived if you have not lain flat on your middle on a thyme lawn."

Thyme grows wild in Europe, from the mountains of Greece to the rolling downs of England and in parts of

Asia and Africa. Bees have always loved this herb, and honey made from thyme is the most delicious and fragrant of all. Thyme was always planted near the bee-hives and the hives were also rubbed with it.

Thyme is very easy to grow; propagate by root division, or strike cuttings in sand in late winter; grow the plants in light, well-drained soil in a sunny position and you will be rewarded by a spreading, thickly foliaged little plant in a very short time.

In spring and summer the scented flowers of the different varieties shade from reddish purple through soft lilac and pink to white. Although each variety has its own individuality of perfume, flavour and form, they are all aromatic. The volatile oil from this herb, thymol, is extracted and used in industry. In Roman times this herb was a remedy for melancholy, and today a tea made from the leaves is regarded as being invigorating and refreshing.

The number of different thymes are too numerous to list, the following varieties being the most easily obtainable at present.

Garden thyme (*Thymus vulgaris*) is the species most often used in flavouring. It is a particularly savoury herb, growing into a shrubby plant about one foot high, with pale, creamy-pink flowers in spring. It dries very successfully; harvest the branches just before the plant flowers and hang up in a shady place for two or three weeks. Rub the dry leaves off the brittle stalks and store in airtight glass jars. The pungency of your own dried thyme surpasses that of any bought kind.

Lemon thyme (*T. citriodorus*) is aptly named, having a delicious lemon scent overlaying the typical thymy flavour. The leaves are softer and rounder than garden thyme, and are therefore more satisfactory to use in cooking when picking sprays straight from the garden; it is also valuable when dried. The plant grows to a height of 12 inches and has fragrant pink flowers in spring and all through the summer, the colour of a moss-rose. It is a hue difficult to describe because it is not the pink we know today, nor is it mauve, but a soft combination of both, delicate, and restful to the eyes.

Variegated thyme (*T. citriodorus variegatus*) has green leaves with white or gold variegation and a definite lemon scent also. It may be used both as an ornamental plant and in cooking; it grows to 12 inches high and has pink flowers.

Carroway thyme (*T. herba-barona*) has a creeping habit and pink flowers. It has an unmistakable scent, redolent of carroway, and may be used in the kitchen to give a subtle flavour to certain food. The leaves stripped from the stalk give a fresh and piquant flavour to sandwiches cut very thinly and spread first with smooth scrambled egg.

T. nitidus is a fascinating little plant particularly suitable for rocky niches and those small spaces that should be left when flagging a terrace. It grows up into a little green hillock, looking rather like a spreading miniature bonsai tree, and in summer it is powdered with pale, mauve-tinted flowers.

T. pauciflorus is a strong-growing carpeting thyme with green foliage and soft pink flowers; it is excellent for rockeries and borders.

T. serpyllum is reputed to be Shakespeare's "wild thyme", and because of its magic associations is a magic herb; Culpeper calls it "Mother of thyme". It has a vigorous creeping habit, is very fragrant and covered with bright pink flowers in summer. It looks most attractive growing around the sundial in a herb garden. This is the variety which is recommended for use in a thyme lawn, and for making a fragrant garden seat by putting earth where you desire your scented seat to be, and then planting the thyme in the early spring to form a dense mat, which it does very quickly.

T. serpyllum coccineous is very similar to the above but with a greater profusion of flowers.

T. serpyllum lanuginosus has tiny woolly leaves, delicately scented. It forms a thick, grey carpet which is most effective for a rockery. It grows nicely on top of a herb-garden wall where it will fall in thin silver strands over the golden stones.

T. serpyllum albus is a carpeting thyme with green foliage and drifts of white flowers in the spring.

Westmoreland thyme grows to two feet with soft mauve flowers. It could be described as Edna Walling's own. She mentions it many times in her books, as for instance: "One of the most perfect of all edging plants is the Westmoreland thyme, a variety of *T. serpyllum* which is mid-way between *T. vulgaris*, the common culinary thyme (an excellent carpeting and edging plant by the way) and the ground clinging *T. serpyllum* known variously as Shepherd's thyme and Mother of thyme."

There are many well-known stuffing and force-meat recipes employing thyme and a sniff of a spray of it will immediately make you think of roast chicken and turkey. The green leaves may be stripped from the stalks and used in place of dried thyme for a change, but the aroma of this herb is more penetrating when dried.

The warm smell of thyme brings to mind a tender chicken roasting in the oven, or perhaps a Christmas turkey, or a fat goose, especially if the thyme is freshly dried and still retains its typical piercing aroma. Thymol, an extract from the plant, is used in cough and digestive medicines.

Thyme tea is a popular beverage in some countries, and is quite delicious. Nicholas Culpeper, the early-17th-century herbalist, says: "A strong infusion, drank as tea, is pleasant, and a very effectual remedy for head-ache, giddiness, and other disorders of that kind; and a certain remedy for that troublesome complaint, the night-mare."

There are certain dishes where a teaspoon or two of thyme alone is called for, and not a combination of herbs. It is used to flavour meat dishes, soups, bread stuffings, forcemeat, and some vegetables such as eggplant, mushrooms, onions, beetroot, zucchini and baby marrows.

BUTTERED MARROW

Peel and slice thinly some fresh young marrows or zucchini. Place in a saucepan with 1 oz. butter, some salt and pepper, and 1 teaspoon dried thyme. Cover, and cook gently till soft. The vegetable must not be allowed to burn in the beginning; if necessary, add a little more butter. The flavour is so delicate that this may be served as an entrée or eaten between courses.

TURKEY STUFFING

This recipe for a stuffing for a 15-lb. roast turkey was given to me by Mr and Mrs R. E. Allen, neighbours whose family have lived in the same district for 120 years. Their old stone house has high, cool ceilings, wide verandas and an old fireplace where a large black saucepan used to hang by a chain and hook.

Grate into a large bowl 8 cups soft breadcrumbs. Rub in ¼ lb. butter, add 1 onion (grated), 3 sticks celery (grated), 1 lb. raw pork (finely minced), the grated rind and juice of a lemon, 1 apple (grated), one 1-lb. tin crushed pineapple (drained), 2 eggs, ½ cup chopped parsley, 1 tablespoon dried thyme, and a little salt and pepper. Mix all ingredients together (the consistency should be crumbly). Before stuffing the bird, rub the cavity with garlic.

The pineapple juice may be mixed with the fat to baste the turkey.

SAVOURY MEAT BALLS IN SAUCE

Sauce: Simmer together for 15 minutes 1½ pints water, 1 onion, 1 bay leaf, a few black peppercorns, a pinch of salt, and 2 beef cubes. Remove the onion and bay leaf. The mixture is now ready for the meat balls (the sauce is thickened at a later stage).

Meat balls: Mix together 1½ lb. sausage mince or mince steak, 1 egg (beaten), 1 onion (finely chopped), 2 teaspoons dried thyme, and a little salt and pepper. With well-floured hands form the mixture into balls and drop them into the sauce. Simmer for 30 minutes. Remove the meat balls and keep them hot in a dish. Thicken the sauce with 1 dessertspoon cornflour blended with a little milk. Add chopped parsley, and pour this sauce over the meat balls. Serve hot.

CHICKEN MOULD

When the weather is hot and days are long and sunny, this smooth chicken mould is fragrant and cooling.

Simmer a chicken. Reserve the stock (about 3 cups). For the béchamel sauce, take 3 cups of chicken stock, melt 3 oz. butter in a saucepan, add 3 tablespoons plain flour, and blend; gradually pour in the stock with 1 cup milk added, stirring continuously. Put the béchamel on one side. Soften 2 envelopes gelatine in ½ cup hot water and stir until dissolved, then add to the béchamel sauce, mixing thoroughly. Add at once the following ingredients: 3 cups cooked chopped chicken, 2 tablespoons finely chopped shallot, 2 tablespoons chopped red capsicum, a little salt and pepper, ½ cup whipped cream, 1 tablespoon lemon juice, 1 teaspoon dried thyme, and ¼ teaspoon nutmeg. Chill until beginning to thicken, turn into a rinsed-out mould, and set in the refrigerator. Unmould onto a flat dish and surround with sprigs of thyme and cress.

THYME STUFFING FOR POULTRY

1 *cup of white bread-crumbs*	*Salt and freshly ground pepper*
2 *oz. butter*	1 *tablespoon thyme*
1 *tablespoon finely chopped onion*	1 *dessertspoon chopped parsley*
Grated rind and juice of 1 *lemon*	1 *dessertspoon chopped marjoram*
	1 *egg*

Soften the onion in a frying pan in the butter without browning. Put all the ingredients in a bowl binding them together with the egg.

RABBIT COOKED IN MILK

1 rabbit
2 tablespoons flour
4 oz. butter or
  1 small cup of oil
2 finely chopped onions

1 pint milk
Salt and pepper
1 tablespoon dried thyme
  or 2 tablespoons fresh
  chopped thyme

Cut the rabbit into pieces and roll in the flour. Heat the butter or oil and gently fry the floured rabbit on both sides. Put the rabbit, onions and thyme in layers in a fireproof dish, seasoning as you go with salt and pepper. Pour in 1 pint of milk, cover the dish and cook in a moderately slow oven for 2 hours.

We have been enjoying this recipe ever since the war years when meat was rationed and rabbit was very popular and cooked in many different ways.

SAVOURY MEAT LOAF

½ lb. minced bacon
1 lb. minced steak
½ cup white breadcrumbs
1 chopped onion
1 egg

2 teaspoons dried thyme or
  1 tablespoon fresh
  chopped thyme
½ cup milk
Salt and pepper

Put the minced steak and bacon into a bowl and add the breadcrumbs, onion, thyme, salt and pepper. Work it well together with a fork, add the milk and the egg, blending the whole mixture. Turn it into a loaf tin and bake in a moderate oven for 1 hour.

HERBAL TEAS

It would be foolish in a book of this size to try to discuss all the medicinal herbs and their uses. The few that have been mentioned are well known for their health-giving qualities.

A herbal tea, or tisane, is an infusion of boiling water and herbs, either fresh or dried, and is usually taken after dinner or before going to bed, with a little lemon and honey added. These teas are more widely known in other countries than in Australia. They are both pleasant to drink and beneficial, often being a remedy for a mild indisposition. Many people assert that taking them over a long period builds up a resistance to a number of illnesses.

In England, particularly in the country, herbal teas still retain their popularity; in France it is the custom to have a tisane on retiring; in America a famous beauty salon serves chamomile tea to help clear the complexion and to soothe the nerves, and the Chinese have known the value of herbal teas for hundreds of years.

It is said that at the end of the day, after the exacting demands of our present life, which distracts the mind and tires the body, a herbal tea unites the spirit and the body again in harmony with oneself and the universe. An infusion of the flower-heads of German chamomile is recommended to bring about this tranquil sensation of well-being.

Some well-known herbal teas are those made of lime-

Sage Bread (p.95).

flowers, orange flowers, lemon-scented verbena leaves, hyssop flowers, bergamot leaves and sage leaves, the last-named herb having once had the reputation of delaying old age. Dried nettle tea is a natural source of iron; rosemary tea is supposed to stimulate the memory; peppermint tea, if taken regularly, helps to ward off colds; mint, lemon-thyme and balm tea in the summer are all refreshing and invigorating, and angelica tea helps digestion.

There are numerous varieties of the chamomile daisy growing in many gardens and superficially they look alike, with their finely cut, fern-like leaves and tiny, white-and-gold daisy flower-heads, but there are differences in appearance and their uses are not the same. It is interesting also to note the different botanical headings under which they are known. The most usual kind found in gardens is the old feverfew or febrifuge, *Chrysanthemum parthenium*, and is not used very much today in herbal teas. It was once considered a cure for headaches. Culpeper says with some asperity, "and if any grumble because they cannot get the herb in winter, tell them, if they please, they may make a syrup of it in summer".

Both the English chamomile (*Anthemis nobilis*), a perennial, and the German chamomile (*Matricaria chamomilla*) an annual, are widely used in herbal teas. There seems to be some difference of opinion among herbal writers as to which is the "true" chamomile, and which has the most efficacy. "Maythen" was the old Saxon name for English chamomile, and the Spaniards call it "manzilla", meaning little apple. A Spanish wine, flavoured with chamomile, is known by the same name; this is also the variety recommended for a chamomile lawn. For tea, only the dried flower-heads are used, and these should be gathered early in the morning and spread

Noodles and Mushrooms
(p.81).

out to dry on paper in a cool, airy place; when dry put the fragrant heads in clean dry screwtop jars.

German chamomile grows to a height of 12 inches and should be planted in a plot by itself and allowed to self-sow as the seed is rather difficult to collect. When the white-and-gold flowers are massed together like this they make a brave show. Harvest and dry the flower-heads in the same way as English chamomile. By the way, there is an old saying that where chamomile grows the plants in the garden will be healthier.

CHAMOMILE TEA (1 CUP)

Measure 1 cup of water into an enamel saucepan and bring to the boil, sprinkle 1 teaspoon of dried chamomile heads into the water, put on the lid and boil for ½ minute. Remove from the stove and leave the lid on for a little longer so that the valuable essence is not lost. Strain into a cup, flavour with a little lemon juice and sweeten with honey if you wish. It is delicious.

PEPPERMINT TEA (2 OR 3 CUPS)

The true Mitcham peppermint (*Mentha piperita officinalis*) is used for this tea and is recommended to take as a prevention against colds. The character of this mint's aroma is warmly pungent, while the other mints have a lighter, more piercing quality. Like the rest of the mint family, peppermint prefers a fairly moist position and room to spread. Snails love this particular mint so be on guard against these marauders. Tea is made from either the fresh or dried leaves: if using fresh leaves, pick a handful from the garden and put them in a crockery teapot, preferably one kept for this purpose, as there is then no taint from ordinary tea present, pour boiling water on to the leaves, cover and leave to infuse for 5 minutes. Sweeten with honey and flavour with lemon. If using the dried leaves, pick a bundle of stalks in the morning after the dew has gone and spread out to dry. When ready strip the leaves from the stems and put in airtight jars. Make the tea in the same way as chamomile tea.

MINT TEAS

Dried or fresh mint may be used, and made in the same way as Peppermint Tea.

SPARKLING MINT TEA

(From *The Coronation Cookery Book*, compiled by the Country Women's Association of N.S.W.)

3 *quarts strong tea*   ¾ *pint lemon juice*
1½ *quarts soda water*   *Mint and ice*
3 *cups castor sugar*

Make tea in the usual way, allow 4 teaspoons tea to a quart of boiling water. Infuse and then strain, add sugar, stand it until cool. Stir in lemon juice to tea, add soda and serve in tall glass jug with a lump of ice. Place sprigs of mint on rim of glass and in the jug. A few berries, green grapes, or a slice of lemon and orange may be added to each jug. This quantity makes 1¼ gallons, suitable for a large party.

This is a refreshing drink to serve at a tennis party.

NETTLE TEA

Nettle (*Urtica dioica*), the "wergulu" of early Saxon writings was with "maythen", chervil and fennel one of the sacred herbs of those days. It contains iron and protein, and a tisane made of the dried leaves infused in the same way as chamomile tea, helps a cold. The green beverage has a rich, smooth flavour tasting of all the good green things which come from the earth, and in my opinion is best on its own without lemon and honey.

ROSEMARY TEA

Pick a fresh sprig of rosemary from the garden and put it in a cup, pour boiling water over, stand a saucer on the top to keep in the fumes and leave to infuse for 5 minutes. If making more than 1 cup, pick several sprigs and make the tea in a crockery teapot.

ANGELICA TEA

Pick a few fresh angelica leaves and put them in a crockery teapot; pour boiling water on to them, cover and leave to infuse for 5 minutes.

121

FRAGRANT GIFTS

IMAGINATION, AND WILLING FINGERS, WHICH NEED NOT BE too nimble, are the main requirements for making many useful and acceptable gifts which originate from the garden.

Thought and care are important in making the article look attractive. Time is another factor; pot-pourri takes time to mature, pomander balls are a little slow but not difficult to make, and, of course, it is necessary to wait for the lavender to dry before putting it into sachets. A scented gift has the quality of conveying the personality of the giver much more than any other present. A pot-pourri can be a very memorable gift, and one that will stir grateful memories in the receiver. Even during the warmest summer day it will scent a room with fresh perfume, and the hotter the day the more scent it will release. The lid must be replaced at night, and the dried fragrant leaves and flowers stirred frequently.

Fragrant powdered orris root is a necessary ingredient in many of the following recipes and it is interesting to know that it comes from the dried root of the white-flowering Florentine iris, *Iris florentina*. And now for a few gift suggestions.

A POMANDER BALL OR CLOVE ORANGE

It is important to select a ripe, thin-skinned orange. Stick it full of cloves, starting from the stalk-end and going round the orange until it is covered, roll it well in a teaspoonful of orris powder and a teaspoonful of cinnamon mixed together, pressing the powder well in. Wrap the orange in tissue paper and put it away in a dark cupboard for a week or two. Press a staple into the top of the orange and tie a small bow to it, or thread a yard of narrow ribbon through the staple so that the pomander may hang from a coathanger in a wardrobe. Corded ribbon in muted shades of either gold, rose, soft blue, lavender or sage green looks particularly attractive with the snuff-brown of the pomander and its old-world appearance.

A clove orange serves two purposes: it helps to keep moths away from drawers, cupboards and linen closets, as well as scenting them. One hung from the china doorknob of a sitting room can look charming. The orange becomes "petrified" and does not decay in any way—it just grows smaller and smaller. Sometimes pomanders ten years old may be seen, still spicily fragrant, as hard as iron, and very, very small.

Here is a delightful poem called "The Clove Orange" by Eleanor Farjeon:

I'll make a clove orange to give to my darling,
I'll make a clove orange to please my delight,
And lay in her coffer to sweeten her linen
And hang by her pillow to sweeten her night.

I'll choose a small orange as round as the moon is,
That ripened its cheek in the sunniest grove,
And when it is dry as a midsummer hayfield
I'll stick it all round with the head of a clove.

To spice the dull sermon in church of a Sunday,
Her orange of cloves in her bag she shall take;
When parson is prosy and eyelids are drowsy,
One sniff at her spice-ball will charm her awake.

And when she walks forth in the highways and byways
Where fevers are prone and infection is rife,
On her palm she shall carry her little clove orange,
A charm against sickness, to guard her sweet life.

And moth shall not haunt her most delicate garment,
Nor spectre her delicate dream in the night,
When she hangs in her chamber her little dried orange
I've studded with cloves to delight my Delight.

LAVENDER BAGS

Many people today make fragrant lavender bags as gifts which are always welcome. For those who have never made them the following simple directions are given:

Pick the lavender heads just before they are in full bloom. Gather them when the dew has gone and before the hot sun has drawn the scent from the blossoms, spread them in a cool airy place to dry, never in direct sunlight because the sun's rays draw out much of the valuable aroma even when picked. When dry, rub the tiny flowers from the stalks and fill your lavender bags. If these are not ready, store the dried lavender in an airtight jar. Lavender-coloured muslin or organdie are favourite materials to use for the bags which are usually drawn in near the top with lavender ribbon tied in a bow. A little silk embroidery enhances the appearance of the sachets. There is scope for the imagination in making lavender bags, and they need not be of the conventional materials and colours—new ideas are always refreshing.

SWEET BAGS

Sweet bags are similar to lavender bags. They are filled with a variety of ingredients, and while lavender bags are used for scenting drawers and linen cupboards, sweet bags may be used not only for this purpose, but for putting under pillows, and hanging on the backs of chairs, where the warmth and pressure from the head releases the perfume. How charmingly thoughtful our grandmothers were, and how unusual and pleasant it would be today for a guest in the spare-room to discover on retiring the fragrance of the sweet bag under her pillow.

The following recipes all are excellent for making sweet bags.

1. Dry equal quantities of lemon-scented geranium and rose-scented geranium leaves. Crumble and mix with the desired amount of dried lavender flowers and a little orris root powder. Fill pastel coloured silk bags.

2. Take 2 handfuls of dried rose petals, and add 2 oz. of orris root powder, a little common salt, 2 oz. of coriander seeds, 2 teaspoons of cinnamon, 1 teaspoon of ground cloves and 1 handful of dried orange blossom. Mix together and fill sachets.

3. Mix 2 handfuls each of dried wallflowers and rosemary flowers, 2 oz. of orris root powder, and 1 teaspoon of powdered nutmeg. Fill bags. This mixture is particularly aromatic and sweet. The rosemary flowers hold their perfume admirably and mingle well with the warm fragrance of wallflowers.

A SCENTED COATHANGER

Make one of the preparations for a sweet sachet or lavender bag and fill a muslin bag the length of a wooden coathanger. Cover the hanger with plain material and sew the filled muslin bag into place on top of the hanger. Cover the hanger completely with a suitable material—silk, sprigged muslin, or georgette in pastel colours are all pretty. Softly pleat the material and cover the hook too. An extra touch may be added by swinging a sweet sachet by a length of ribbon from the centre of the hanger.

GIFT PACKAGES

A gift package of home-dried culinary herbs is a welcome present for a friend who is interested in cooking. Cover an old chocolate box or shoe box with pretty wallpaper, preferably one suited to this type of gift, patterned with leaves or flowers, and pack it with small airtight glass jars filled with separate herbs, carefully labelling each one. Paint a leaf or flower on the jar, too, if you wish; the manner in which each person expresses himself is individual and original. A gift package of the tea herbs may be prepared in the same way.

ROSEMARY RUBBING LOTION

Buy 1 pint of odourless rubbing alcohol from the chemist. Put crushed rosemary leaves and flowers, and the highly aromatic seeds, too, if you have them, into a jar. Pour the spirit over, cover and leave for two or three weeks, shaking occasionally. Strain and use. This makes a welcome gift for someone ill in bed. It has a much more pleasant smell than methylated spirit. This recipe may be followed in the same way with other sweet-scented and pungent herbs and flowers, such as lavender, lemon verbena, balm, mint, rose petals, violets, carnations and scented-leaved geraniums.

AROMATICS FOR THE BATH

Sprigs of rosemary are said to be invigorating additions to a bath. A gift package may be made in the way as described for culinary herbs. Fill small individual bags of plain coloured muslin with rosemary, pine needles, lavender heads, dried orange flowers and dried eau-de-Cologne mint, naming each herb on the muslin with a marking pencil; these bags are put into a hot bath and allowed to infuse.

SCENTED NOTE-PAPER

Buy a box of white or pastel note-paper and envelopes and slip the sweet-bag mixture in small sachets between the layers of paper and envelopes. Re-wrap the box in cellophane with narrow ribbon finished with a sachet and ribbon-loops on the top. It does not take long for the perfume to permeate the paper.

Here are some old recipes from *The Scented Garden* by E. S. Rohde:

HONEY SOAP

Take four ounces of white soap and as much honey, half an ounce of salt of tartar, and two or three drachms of the distilled Water of fumitory; mix the whole together. This soap cleanses the skin well, and renders it delicately white and smooth. It is also used advantageously to efface the marks of burns and scalds. ("The Toilet of Flora".)

SCENTED CANDLES

Take Benjamin, storax, of each foure ounces, Frankincense, Olibanum, of each twelve ounces, Labdanum eighteen ounces, Nigella an ounce, Coriander seeds, Juniper berries, of each halfe an ounce; liquid Storax sixe ounces, Turpentine halfe an ounce, forme them into Candles with gum: dragant and Rose water. (*The Charitable Physitian*, by Philibert Guibert, Physitian Regent in Paris, 1639.)

SPICES

ALLSPICE

Allspice comes from a tropical tree that is native to America and is also cultivated in the West Indies and Jamaica. The small sun-dried berries are sometimes known as pimento or Jamaica pepper, but are usually called allspice because the aroma and taste seem to be a combination of cinnamon, cloves, and nutmeg. Allspice is not a mixture of these three spices, as is sometimes thought.

Ground allspice is used in many spice blends and as a flavouring for various cakes, soups, meat dishes, milk puddings and vegetables. The berries are often tied in a muslin bag for use in the making of preserves, pickles, and chutney. Ground allspice with cinnamon helps to give pot-pourri its spicy fragrance.

SPICED VEAL ROLL

1 shoulder of veal, boned
1 cup soft breadcrumbs
1 dessertspoon seeded
  raisins
Grated rind of an orange
2 teaspoons mixed herbs
A few pieces of butter
1 dessertspoon chopped
  shallot or onion
Salt and pepper
4 tablespoons butter or
  margarine
1 teaspoon ground allspice
Orange juice

Mix together the breadcrumbs, raisins, orange rind, herbs, pieces of butter, and shallot. Season with salt and pepper. Roll the meat up with this stuffing in the centre, tie with string, and rub the surface with butter and 1 teaspoon ground allspice. Put in a baking dish with 4 tablespoons fat (butter or margarine) and the juice from the grated orange. Bake in a moderate oven (350° to 375°F.), basting frequently. (If the liquid is reducing too much, add a little stock or water.) Allow 25 minutes to the lb. and 25 minutes over. If the liquid is too thin it may be thickened with a little flour, then poured over the veal, or served separately in a gravy boat.

FRIED ORANGE SLICES

Cut the pithy ends from oranges and discard. Slice the fruit into thin rounds and cover both sides with a mixture of sugar and ground allspice. Melt some butter or margarine and gently fry the orange slices in it, turning until the rinds are lightly browned. Serve hot with roast duck, rabbit, veal, or pork.

ROSE CREAMS

Delicious with black coffee after dinner, this exquisite and rather exotic fondant brings a little of the Golden Road to Samarkand into the recipe collection: ". . . I will make her sweets like flowers. I will perfume my sweets with the perfume of roses, so that she shall say 'a rose'! and smell before she tastes. . . ." (*Hassan*, by James Elroy Flecker).

½ lb. icing sugar	*A few drops of rose water*
1 teaspoon ground allspice	*(obtainable from the*
1 egg white	*pharmacist)*
	Red food colouring

Sift the icing sugar with the allspice. Beat the egg white slightly, and gradually add half the spiced icing sugar, beating well, then the rosewater and enough colouring to make a rosy pink. Add the rest of the icing sugar, to make a stiff consistency. Roll the fondant out on a flat board that has been sprinkled with icing sugar. Cut into rounds with a small cutter and leave to harden.

ROSE GERANIUM JELLY

This is a special preserve in the same mood as Rose Creams: delicately scented, ruby coloured, and glistening, it may be put on the table with roast baby lamb, veal, or poultry; or spread it on thin slices of bread-and-butter.

1 *small bunch of rose*
  geranium leaves
  (about ½ pint)
5 *cups sugar*
1 *teaspoon whole allspice*

Juice of 2 small lemons,
  or 1 large lemon
4 *cups water*
4 *oz. powdered pectin*
Red food colouring

Wash the rose geranium leaves and steep them in the sugar, allspice, and lemon juice for 1 hour. Place in a saucepan with the water and bring to the boil. Strain, add the pectin, and boil again, stirring for about a minute. Add the food colouring. Pour into small clean jars with a rose geranium leaf in each one. Seal the jars.

CAYENNE

Cayenne pepper is the ground product from various species of dried capsicum or red chili pepper. It is cultivated in the East Indies, Africa, and many other parts of the world, in temperate as well as tropical zones. This is an ornamental plant, bearing small, brilliant pods of vermilion fruit. An excellent culinary spice, cayenne also has digestive properties.

Cayenne pepper is extremely hot and so it must be used sparingly. A small amount is invaluable in cheese dishes, sauces, egg dishes, and with shellfish. Cayenne is stimulating and zestful, and is a classic ingredient in a Newburg Sauce.

NEWBURG SAUCE

3 tablespoons butter	2 cups thin cream
3 tablespoons plain flour	or top milk
1 teaspoon paprika	3 egg yolks, slightly beaten
A pinch of cayenne	1 tablespoon sherry
	Salt

Melt the butter in a saucepan. Blend in the flour, paprika, and cayenne. Add the cream gradually, stirring until the mixture thickens. Pour a little of this sauce onto the egg yolks, mix well, and return the mixture to the saucepan. Add sherry, and a pinch of salt. Carefully reheat, stirring constantly (do not boil). Add the cooked lobster pieces, prawns, or scallops, and heat them through. Transfer to a hot dish and serve immediately with steaming rice; or serve with triangles of hot buttered toast.

Spiced Veal Roll (p.131).

CHEESE STRAWS

¼ lb. butter	Cayenne
1 cup plain flour	Salt
3 tablespoons grated cheese	1 egg yolk

Rub the butter, flour, and cheese together, season with salt and add the egg yolk. If the mixture is too stiff, moisten with a little water. Roll out and cut into strips, forming three or four of them into circles. Bake in a hot oven (400°F.) for about 15 minutes. When the cheese straws are cool, slip them in bundles into the circles.

EGG AND POTATO PIE

Peel and boil some potatoes and whip them until creamy with butter, milk, a little salt and pepper, and a grated onion. Spread thickly in a buttered ovenproof dish. Break an egg into a cup and slide it gently onto the potato; repeat, covering the potato with as many eggs as required. Mask the eggs with a little cream or top milk, and sprinkle with salt and cayenne. Bake in a medium-hot oven (380°F.) until the whites are set and the yolks are still soft-looking.

TOMATO DUMPLINGS

4 oz. self-raising flour	1 dessertspoon chopped
A walnut-sized piece of	parsley (optional)
butter	6 tablespoons tomato juice
1 dessertspoon grated	¼ teaspoon salt
cheese	A pinch of cayenne

This is another delicious recipe from my neighbour Mrs R. E. Allen.

Sift the flour with the salt and cayenne, rub in the butter, add the cheese and, if liked, some chopped parsley. Stir in the tomato juice, making a very soft scone dough. Drop spoonfuls on top of a prepared favourite stew a little time before it is ready to serve (say 15 minutes)—putting the lid on and letting the dumplings cook gently for 12 to 15 minutes.

Bortsch (p.144).

CHILI POWDER

Chili powder may be a mixture of dried ground chili peppers, aromatic seeds, spices, and herbs or it may be the ground peppers unmixed; the flavour differs with the manufacturers' formulas, and varies from mildly hot to very hot. The quantity of chili powder given in these recipes will vary with the brand you buy. At first it is better to use a little less than too much.

Cayenne, cumin, and oregano are often added in the preparation of the blend. The best and hottest chili powder comes from small bright red chilis known as bird's-eye peppers. Originally this spice came from Mexico where the Aztecs introduced them to the conquering Spaniards in the sixteenth century.

The aroma of the powder is fiercely peppery, the colour being a rust red and the flavour hot and glowing. Its traditional use is in Chile con Carne, a Mexican dish, but it has become indispensable in the making of certain sauces and in the blending of some curry powders.

When used prudently, chili powder sharpens the flavour of egg dishes, soups, and vegetables, and is particularly good as a flavouring in baked beans.

BARBECUE BAKED BEANS

Two 1-lb. tins baked beans
4 medium-sized to large
   tomatoes
2 onions
1 clove of garlic
1 tablespoon brown sugar

2 tablespoons butter or
   margarine
1 teaspoon mustard powder
1 dessertspoon chili
   powder
Salt

Pour boiling water onto the tomatoes, skin them, and chop coarsely. Peel and slice the onions and garlic and cook in the melted butter until soft. Add the brown sugar, mustard powder, chili powder, and some salt to taste. Cook until mushy (about 10 minutes), add the baked beans, and cook a little longer. Serves 8.

CHILE CON CARNE

A fiery dish to take the place of curry for a change. Legend says that the Aztecs showed the *conquistadores* how to make it.

2 lb. lean steak, chopped into cubes
Two 10-oz. tins red kidney beans
1 large tin tomatoes, or 3 cups tomato pieces
3 tablespoons vegetable oil
2 onions, peeled and chopped
2 cloves of garlic, chopped
2 tablespoons chili powder
2 tablespoons plain flour
1 teaspoon oregano
1 teaspoon cumin seed
2 teaspoons salt

Heat the oil in an enamelled fireproof dish or a thick saucepan, add the onion and garlic, and cook until soft. Add the chili powder and meat, turning the meat until it is evenly browned. Blend in the flour, then add the tomato pieces (including liquid), oregano, and cumin. Cover, and simmer for 1 hour. Add the beans and salt, and cook for a further 15 minutes.

Chile con Carne (meaning chili with meat) is improved if made a day in advance: the spices will have truly permeated the meat, gravy, and beans. Serve hot with a crisp green salad and some icy-cold beer. For special occasions a wine from Alsace, Gewurztraminer, is suggested: its powerful bouquet is a fit companion for the hot Chile con Carne.

MEXICAN GUACAMOLE

Mash one ripe avocado pear until creamy, incorporate one small grated onion, one small, peeled, finely chopped tomato, a few drops of olive oil, and a pinch each of oregano, salt and chili powder. Place in a dish, with the stone of the avocado embedded in the mixture to prevent discoloration, and chill. Serve on a large lettuce leaf, as a savoury dip, with potato chips or plain biscuits.

CINNAMON

This spice, which comes from a tree native to Ceylon and Malabar, has been highly esteemed from remote times for its preservative and medicinal qualities, and as a flavouring for food and beverages.

When the trees are grown commercially the tender bark is peeled from the numerous long, slender shoots, and it curls into quills or sticks which are then dried in the sun. The fragrance of the bark comes from an essential oil, oil of cinnamon, which has valuable medicinal uses.

The dried bark from a cassia tree is also known as cinnamon, and is similar in flavour and appearance.

Cinnamon is used either whole or powdered. Ground cinnamon mixed with sugar on hot buttered toast is an old favourite; buttered tea cake strewn with sugar and cinnamon is always eaten down to the last delectable, spiced crumb. Ground cinnamon gives liveliness to milk puddings, mulled wines, chutneys, and cakes, and to various vegetables and stewed fruits. Combined with other spices it is a traditional ingredient in Christmas cakes, mince pies, and Christmas puddings, and is also one of the spices that go into the blending of curry powder.

Cinnamon sticks are used in a variety of ways: stirring black coffee with a piece of cinnamon gives it an Eastern aura, while on a bleak night a hot rum toddy flavoured with a little sugar and a twist of lemon peel and spiked with aromatic cinnamon sticks is most comforting, especially after a long journey.

In 1815 a tooth-powder was made by mixing "½ oz. powdered cinnamon and ½ oz. well-prepared chalk well together". This is one of the "receipts" in *Lotions and Potions*.

TREACLE TART

As old-fashioned as caraway comfits and syllabubs, or pot-pourri and beeswax candles, this delightful tart is as welcome today as it ever was—if one is fortunate enough to come across it. A sprinkling of cinnamon over the top, although not always traditional, is a pleasing addition. The pastry for this sweet is excellent when made with fine wholemeal flour instead of refined white flour.

SHORT PASTRY

2 cups wholemeal flour
1 teaspoon baking powder
A pinch of salt
2 oz. butter or margarine
¼ cup cold water

FILLING

3 tablespoons golden syrup
1 dessertspoon lemon juice
Grated lemon rind
3 tablespoons soft white breadcrumbs
1 teaspoon ground cinnamon

Sift the flour, baking powder and salt. Rub in the butter. Add enough water to make a stiff dough. Roll out on a floured board. Line a greased flat pie-plate with the pastry, pricking well all over.

For the filling, measure the syrup into a saucepan with a hot tablespoon (this makes the measuring easier), add the lemon juice, grated rind, and breadcrumbs. Warm slightly over low heat, pour into the pastry case, sprinkle with the cinnamon, and bake in a moderate oven (350° to 375°F.) for 25 minutes. Serve cold with cream.

DEVONSHIRE JUNKET

An old recipe from *Good English Food* by Florence White, this has been altered slightly to suit ingredients available today.

Mix together in a bowl 1 tablespoon sugar, 1 tablespoon brandy or rum, ½ teaspoon ground cinnamon, and 2 crushed junket tablets. Pour onto these 1 pint warm milk. Allow to set, then spread ¼ pint whipped cream over the top and sprinkle with sugar. "When well made, junket should cut into smooth shiny slices like jelly. Unlike jelly, it will set better and more quickly in a room of ordinary temperature than a cold larder."

FLAMING BANANAS

A lighted dessert is always exciting. This recipe is delicious as well.

Allow 2 bananas for each person. Peel and halve, place in a shallow fireproof dish, sprinkle with lemon juice, strew with sugar and cinnamon, and dot liberally with butter. Place under a medium-hot grill, and when soft and golden bring to the table and pour over 2oz. rum, and ignite it.

SWEET-SOUR BROWN BEANS

1 *lb. brown beans or haricot beans*	¼ *cup cider vinegar*
	1 *tablespoon golden syrup*
2 *pints water*	2 *teaspoons salt*
¼ *cup brown sugar*	*A piece of cinnamon stick*

This is an excellent dish to serve with meat, or with crisp bacon for breakfast.

Wash the beans, cover with the water, and soak overnight. Do not change the water. Simmer next day for 30 minutes or until the beans are soft. Add the rest of the ingredients, and cook slowly with the lid off, stirring occasionally, for a further 30 minutes or until tender. Serve piping hot.

1¾ cups plain flour
¼ cup self-raising flour
½ lb. butter
½ cup raw sugar
½ cup best honey
5 eggs
1 level teaspoon of each of these: salt, ground cinnamon, ground cloves, ground allspice, nutmeg

Juice and grated rind of 1 lemon
¼ lb. of each of these: glacé cherries, sultanas, stoned raisins, crystallized pineapple, glacé figs, mixed peel, crystallized papaw, shelled almonds
1 sherry glass of rum (or the same amount of orange juice)

Prepare the fruit, halving the nuts and cherries and chopping the bigger fruit into small cubes. Sift the flours and spices together, and mix a small portion of this sifted spiced flour with the fruit. Cream the butter and sugar, add the honey, the eggs one at a time, and the lemon juice and grated rind. Fold in the sifted spiced flour, then the fruit, and lastly the rum or orange juice. Put into an 8-inch baking tin which has been lined with two thicknesses of brown paper (the inner layer oiled with butter). Bake in a slow oven (300°F.) for 3 to 4 hours. Weight when cooked is about 4 lb.

CLOVES

Whole cloves are the dried flower-buds of an aromatic evergreen tree that is native to the Molucca Islands and is grown today in many hot countries. The pungent clove, either whole or ground, has become a necessary flavouring in a number of dishes. The volatile oil of cloves, a powerful antiseptic, is familiar to everyone.

The name clove is derived from the Latin word *clavus*, meaning nail, which the clove resembles in form.

A deliciously scented clove orange hung in the clothes closet was extremely popular a few centuries ago for repelling insects. (*See Fragrant Gifts p. 122 for instructions on making a clove orange.*)

Held to the nostrils, a clove orange allayed the more offensive odours of the times. "It is not surprising that Cardinal Wolsey, when he ventured either into the lower regions of his own residence or risked the pervasive odours of the streets of London, commonly carried a spice-ball. . . ." (*A Tudor Tragedy*, by Lacey Baldwin Smith.)

Whole cloves are used as a flavouring in many kinds of preserves, mulled wines, stewed fruits, meat dishes, and soups. For stews or soups simmer with the other ingredients a whole onion studded with cloves and remove it before serving. Drop a clove into the hollowed-out centre of a cooking-apple, pack with butter and brown sugar, and bake in a moderate oven (350°F.) until tender.

When boiling fresh salt pork ("poor man's bacon") add to the water a few cloves, together with some peppercorns, a pinch of thyme, and a bay leaf. Simmer for about

2 hours, allow to cool in the water, drain, and keep chilled. The delicate texture of the pork permeated with the herbs and spices is often preferred to bacon.

A baked leg of ham, crumbed and studded with whole cloves and preserved pineapple, is a traditional favourite. A friend's large ham was treated in much the same way one Christmas Eve, with the effective and festive addition of red and green glacé cherries impaled on wooden picks —its tempting appearance resulted in our own ham being dealt with in a similar fashion immediately! The method is given in this chapter.

Clove-spiced hot pineapple cut in slices and eaten with barbecued meat or served with pork or ham is excellent: stud a carefully peeled pineapple with cloves and cook on a rotisserie (if you have one in your stove), or spike through the centre with a long skewer and turn slowly over the barbecue coals. Baste with melted butter and orange juice until well glazed and heated through.

Ground cloves are included in numerous recipes, such as fruit cake, buns, mincemeat, milk puddings, and various sauces and vegetable dishes.

FESTIVE HAM

This recipe for garnishing a ham was given to me by a friend, Mrs R. R. Beck, whose ham I have described a little earlier in this chapter. The garnish may be applied either to cooked fresh ham or to tinned ham; it gives the meat an attractive, mouth-watering appearance and adds a delightful flavour.

If using a tinned ham, remove it carefully from the tin and put on a large plate or board. Remove every vestige of gelatine coating, and score the top deeply in a diamond pattern. With floured hands gently rub and pat flour all over the surface until it is quite dry, then stud the centre of each diamond with cloves.

Open a tin of pineapple rings, and drain them. Put the juice into a saucepan to heat, together with a generous portion of butter. (For the largest ham, 2 big tins of pineapple will be needed, and ½ lb. butter.)

Make a mixture of dry breadcrumbs, flour, brown sugar, and some dry mustard, add enough hot pineapple mixture to make a thick paste, and spread a portion all over the top and sides of the ham. Lift it into a baking dish lined with buttered foil, put into a hot oven (about 400°F.) and let it heat through for 10 to 15 minutes. Remove from the oven, and with a knife or spatula spread the remaining paste on the top and sides.

Spear red and green glacé cherries with wooden picks, putting one through each pineapple ring and onto the ham. Do this in a pleasing pattern around the sides first, then on the top, with the remaining cherries clustered together.

Return the ham to the oven for 20 minutes, allowing the coating to become crusty, then during the last 20 minutes baste frequently with the pineapple and butter, which must be kept bubbling on the stove. When all the liquid has been used, remove the ham from the oven and allow it to cool.

APPLE PUDDING

This is essentially a family pudding; it is a simple recipe, and nourishing. The quantity given is quite large, so there should be enough for "seconds". Have plenty of cream on the table.

Peel, slice, and core enough cooking apples to thickly cover the bottom of a buttered baking dish; add 4 or 5 whole cloves and 2 tablespoons seedless raisins, sprinkle with lemon juice, and strew with sugar. Pour over this a batter made with 2 cups plain flour, a pinch of salt, ½ cup sugar, 2 eggs, and 1 pint milk. Bake in a moderate oven (350°F.) for 1 hour.

BORTSCH

Make a good rich stock with 2 lb. beef bones and a knuckle of veal covered with water, 1 medium-sized carrot, 1 parsnip, 2 tomatoes (chopped), salt, a little sugar, peppercorns, a bay-leaf, thyme, and an onion stuck with cloves.

After it has simmered for 2 or 3 hours strain it through a colander and return it to the pot, adding 4 raw grated beet-root. Simmer for 10 minutes. The quantity should now be from 3 to 4 pints.

In summer put the soup into a bowl in the refrigerator. If it does not jell overnight, dissolve gelatine in some hot water, stir into the soup, and chill. Serve jellied and icy cold with a spoonful of cream on each serving, and a dusting of ground cloves.

In winter omit the gelatine, add chopped frankfurts, and serve hot.

Vatroushki should be eaten with Bortsch: Tania, a friend of Russian extraction, has given her recipe, and having eaten these delicious little pies in her house I can warmly recommend them. They may accompany other vegetable soups or winter stews.

VATROUSHKI

Make your favourite short pastry, or the following: Sift together 2 oz. self-raising flour, 4 oz. plain flour, a pinch of salt, and 1 dessertspoon sugar. Rub in 4 oz. butter or margarine, add cold water, and mix to a stiff dough. Now mix together ½ lb. cream cheese, 1 egg, 1 tablespoon sugar, a pinch of salt, and 2 tablespoons plain flour. Roll the pastry fairly thinly and cut out circles with a teacup or large glass. Place a spoonful of filling in the centre of each pastry circle, and fold into envelopes, pinching to secure. Brush each with beaten white of egg and bake on a tray for about 20 minutes in a moderate oven (350° to 375°F.).

CURRY POWDER

The word "curry" immediately brings to mind spicy and colourful dishes from sun-drenched Eastern countries where "the dawn comes up like thunder" and on the air is the sound of "tinkly temple-bells".

In these countries, with their hot climates, a way of preparing food has been evolved that is suitable for the comfortable and healthy functioning of the body: it is said, for instance, that many of the hotter spices have a purifying effect on the intestines, and also that in humid, muggy weather curries help to "air-condition" the body.

Curry powder is not one spice but a blend of many spices which when combined with food gives it a unique flavour. In India each family grinds its own choice of aromatic seeds nearly every day. Flavours vary considerably from mild, medium, and sweet to very hot, all depending on which spices, and how many, are used in each blend. Instead of a powder, curry paste is sometimes preferred, in which case the prepared powder, perhaps with different spices and herbs added, is usually moistened with vinegar, pulverized garlic and vegetable oil, then cooked gently for a few minutes and sealed down.

Curry blends vary widely in different countries: Indonesian curry is fiercer as a rule than Indian curry, which to my mind, although hot, is extremely aromatic.

Chicken, rabbit, meat, fish, shellfish, vegetables, and hard-boiled eggs are any one of the main ingredients of a curry dish.

Accompaniments: Plenty of carefully cooked rice accompanies a curry, as well as relishes, which may number from three or four dishes to a great number. The traditional few are mango chutney, grated fresh coconut, or dried, desiccated coconut, shredded Bombay duck (which is a tasty cured fish), and Indian mint sauce, a refreshing and delicious combination of mint leaves and an onion minced together. Fresh coriander leaves are a popular garnish for a curry.

Curry powder: It is interesting to blend your own curry powder and to determine, yourself, the degree of heat and nuances of flavour. The recipe given here is intended to serve as a guide. Turmeric may be omitted and the same quantity of paprika used in its place, some people preferring the taste and colour. A little-known aromatic seed which is essential in the preparation of a curry blend is fenugreek. The small irregularly-shaped seeds are light golden-brown in colour, with a pleasantly bitter flavour and a warm, spicy scent.

An electric blender, grinding machine, or pestle-and-mortar may be used for the mixing and grinding of the powder and seeds. If desired, start from the beginning with the whole spice instead of the ground product: however, most spices bought already ground are simpler to use, and if the quality is good the result is satisfactory.

1 *dessertspoon ground cinnamon*
1 *teaspoon ground cloves*
1 *dessertspoon ground ginger*
1 *dessertspoon fenugreek seed*

1 *dessertspoon mustard seed*
1 *tablespoon chili powder*
1 *tablespoon ground coriander*
1 *tablespoon turmeric*
1 *dessertspoon cumin seed*
2 *teaspoons cardamom seed*

Grind and blend all ingredients together. Keep in an airtight jar. A few whole cloves may be added—they help to perfume the blend deliciously.

Ghee, which is clarified butter, is now available and is recommended as a shortening for the frying of the ingredients, although peanut oil may be used instead.

1 *lb. trimmed beef or lamb, cut into cubes*	2 *or 3 tomatoes, chopped*
3 *tablespoons ghee or peanut oil*	2 *teaspoons salt*
	1 *to 2 tablespoons curry powder*
1 *onion, chopped*	2 *tablespoons plain flour*
4 *cloves of garlic, chopped*	¼ *pint stock*
1 *apple, chopped*	1 *tablespoon golden syrup*
2 *inches ginger root, peeled and sliced*	1 *oz. sultanas*
	1 *lemon, cut in half*

Heat the ghee or oil in a frying pan, and add the onion, garlic, apple, and ginger root. Fry gently until softened. Add the tomato, cook a little longer, then stir in the salt and curry powder. Fry for a few minutes. Transfer the contents of the frying pan to a heavy saucepan, add the meat and flour, and cook till brown. Gradually pour in the stock, then stir in the golden syrup, together with the sultanas and lemon halves. Turn the heat very low, put a lid on the saucepan, and simmer for 2 hours, stirring occasionally. About 15 minutes before serving, pick up the lemon halves with the kitchen tongs and squeeze them so that the juice goes into the curry (discard the lemon halves when this has been done). Serve with rice and accompaniments.

INDONESIAN CURRY

Accompaniments: With this curry serve the rice individually moulded for each person. Press the cooked rice into cups and then unmould immediately. (The rice may be kept hot by standing the cups in a covered shallow pan of gently boiling water before unmoulding it.) As many side dishes as you wish may be prepared, as long as they include prawn crisps, fried bananas, hot chutney, and very small meat balls.

Coconut milk: The liquid used in Indonesian curry is coconut milk, which is not the milk from the inside of this nut but an infusion of grated coconut and water. It is made by pouring hot water onto desiccated coconut, the quantities usually being 3 tablespoons of coconut to 1 cup of water. After the coconut has been soaking for 1 hour or more, strain the liquid through a muslin cloth and gently squeeze the residue through the cloth to extract the goodness and flavour. A lesser quantity of grated fresh coconut to the same amount of water may be used instead.

HOT CHICKEN CURRY

Substitute fish or meat for the chicken in this recipe if you wish. This dish improves with keeping and should be made the day before it is to be eaten.

> 1 *small chicken, disjointed and cut up*
> 2 *tablespoons peanut oil*
> 1 *onion, chopped*
> 2 *cloves of garlic, chopped*
> 2 *tablespoons peanut butter*
> 2 *teaspoons salt*
> 1 *pint coconut milk (see the preceding recipe)*

SPICE MIXTURE

> 1 *tablespoon chili powder*
> 1 *dessertspoon ground cumin*
> 1 *dessertspoon turmeric*
> 1 *dessertspoon ground coriander*
> 1 *dessertspoon ground ginger*
> 2 *lemon or lime leaves*

Warm the oil in a saucepan, and fry the onion and garlic in it until soft. Add the peanut butter and the salt. Mix the spices together in a small dish and add 2 or 3 tablespoons of them to the mixture in the saucepan. Add the flour. Stir and cook until well blended. Gradually pour in the coconut milk, stirring all the time. Add the chicken, then the lemon leaves, and simmer for 2 hours. Serve with rice and accompaniments.

PAPAW PICKLE

From Mathilde's *Island Recipe Book*, compiled in the New Hebrides by the women living there, comes this curry-flavoured papaw pickle.

Cut 1 lb. green tomatoes into small pieces, sprinkle well with salt, and leave overnight. Next day, cut into small pieces a small, very green papaw (first removing the seeds), 3 cucumbers, 2 onions, and 9 small chilis. Mix with the tomato, adding 5 teaspoons of brown sugar and 4 teaspoons of good curry powder. Cover with vinegar and boil till soft. Bottle.

GINGER

Ginger is a native of tropical Asia, grown also in Africa, India, China, and Jamaica. The perennial root is tuberous and creeping; after the plant has died down, the root is dried and then preserved in syrup, or it is crystallized or ground.

Ginger is an important ingredient in the blending of curry powder, and its rich, clean tang has been appreciated for hundreds of years in many different kinds of food. Whole pieces in syrup sealed in pretty blue-and-white or other attractively coloured patterned jars from the Orient have been a favourite of mine since childhood. In its crystallized, sugary form ginger makes a pungent sweetmeat, and small pieces added to the ingredients give added flavour to rich spice cakes.

Green ginger is sometimes called for in recipes: this is usually available canned and preserved in liquid. Pieces of the whole root are used in marinades for teriyaki (a recipe for Beef Teriyaki is given in this section), in pickles and chutney, in Chinese food, and in some recipes for ginger beer and ginger wine. Ground ginger may nearly always be substituted for the whole root if necessary, and in this form it is used in ginger beer, ginger snaps, gingerbread, sauces, spice cakes, preserves, and sweets, and to flavour certain meat and vegetable dishes.

Every household has its favourite spices and its favourite containers for them. We still have a pepper shaker with ginger in it which belonged to my grandfather. Sometimes we take it out of the cabinet and shake it over

150

French Ice Cream (p.205).

apple pie, just as he did. The ginger still has a bite and mellowness about it, and happy moments are re-lived as the gleaming little container is passed round the table.

Gingerbread men and other gingerbread fancies were sold at country fairs in England in olden days. Flora Thompson gives us a glimpse of highdays and holidays of the past in her *Lark Rise to Candleford*. Of one feast-day holiday she writes: "The women made their houses very clean and neat for Feast Monday, and, with hollyhocks nodding in at the open windows and a sight of the clean, yellow stubble of the cleared fields beyond, and the hum of friendly talk and laughter within, the tea parties were very pleasant. At the beginning of the 'eighties the outside world remembered Fordlow Feast to the extent of sending one old woman with a gingerbread stall. On it were gingerbread babies with currants for eyes. . . ."

MANGO MOUSSE

The incomparable taste of mangoes is enhanced by the ginger in this sweet with the tropical fragrance.

2 large ripe mangoes
1 cup water
½ cup sugar
1 teaspoon ground ginger
1 envelope gelatine (dissolved in ¼ cup hot water)
2 eggs, separated
½ pint cream, whipped

Simmer the water, sugar, and ginger together for a few minutes. Peel and slice the mangoes, add to the syrup, and poach until soft. Sieve them (syrup included) or put into a blender. Add the dissolved gelatine and return the mixture to the saucepan with the egg yolks. Stir over low heat until smooth and thickened (do not boil). Remove from the stove, cool slightly, and fold in the whipped cream and the beaten egg whites. Pour into a bowl or into individual dishes. Chill. Just before serving, cover the top with shredded coconut (for extra flavour and crispness brown the coconut beforehand in the oven).

151

Mango Mousse (p.151).

A quick, uncomplicated recipe when tomatoes are plentiful. The ground ginger and chili powder give an invigorating flavour to this relish.

6 *lb. red tomatoes*	2 *teaspoons ground ginger*
2 *onions*	1 *teaspoon ground mace*
2 *cloves of garlic*	1 *rounded dessertspoon*
1 *lb. raw or brown sugar*	*chili powder*
1 *cup herb or cider vinegar*	1 *dessertspoon dried*
2 *oz. common salt*	*oregano*

Thickening:

2 tablespoons plain flour and some vinegar

Pour some boiling water onto the tomatoes and leave for a few minutes. Drain the water off. Peel and chop the tomatoes. Peel and slice the onions and garlic. Put all ingredients except the thickening together into a saucepan and boil gently for 30 minutes. Blend the flour with enough vinegar to make a thin paste, pour into the mixture, and boil for a further 15 minutes, stirring all the time. Cool, then seal the relish in jars.

BEEF TERIYAKI

The steak in this recipe may be replaced by pork, veal, or chicken.

1½ *lb. rump steak, cut into 2-inch squares*
1 *medium-sized tin pineapple rings, cut into*
quarters
1 *small jar stuffed olives*
Red glacé cherries

MARINADE

1 *clove garlic, crushed*
¼ *cup soy sauce*
1 *teaspoon ground ginger*
1 *tablespoon sherry*
Juice from pineapple rings

Combine the ingredients for the marinade. Add the steak, leaving it to soak for 1 hour. Now thread alternately on

6-inch metal skewers the meat, pineapple pieces, olives, and cherries. Grill, turning frequently and basting with the marinade. Allow 2 or 3 skewers for each person. Serve with boiled rice and a green salad.

For a barbecue, increase the quantities and thread on very long skewers, adding some or all of the following: mushrooms, small onions or pickled onions, capsicum slices, stoned prunes, thickly sliced dill cucumbers, gherkins, wedges of tomato, and some stoned black olives. Rest the skewers over the coals, turning them until the food is cooked.

MACE AND NUTMEG

Mace and nutmeg are grouped together because they both come from the same thirty-foot tropical tree, which grows in the Molucca Islands, Ceylon, Sumatra, and Malaya. In some countries the species are different, and accordingly the shape and flavour of the fruit varies.

Imagine a section of the fruit cut in half: first there is the outer covering or shell, then the scarlet network or aril, which when dried is known as mace; within this lacy covering is the nutmeg.

The flavours of mace and nutmeg are very similar, mace being more piercingly aromatic. If mace is difficult to obtain, nutmeg may be substituted.

Nutmeg

Nutmeg usually comes to us ground, but the hard, dried seed may be kept in a small jar and grated when required. In former days every household had its nutmeg grater and its whole nutmegs. This spice has a pleasing and rather crisp, dry quality, and is often included in rich food. An egg flip or eggnog is not complete without a sprinkling of nutmeg on the top: besides having an agreeable flavour, nutmeg is supposed to have a soothing effect on the digestive system. It is interesting to read that its use in medicine is "as a stimulant and carminative". (A carminative is a medicine to cure colic or flatulence.) The flavour of nutmeg does not dominate when mixed with other herbs and spices.

Ground or freshly grated nutmeg flavours milk puddings, cakes, biscuits, soups, breads, oyster and fish dishes, pumpkin pie, cream sauces, some meat dishes, and nearly all beverages made with milk.

Mace

The origin of mace has just been described. It may be obtained ground or whole. When whole it is known as a "blade" of mace. The colour of dried mace.is more golden than that of nutmeg, and the flavour is stronger, therefore a smaller quantity is required in cooking. Mace in a Sauce Suprême for fish is excellent. It is often called for in pickle and chutney recipes, in cheese dishes, to give character to creamed spinach, steamed young carrots, and mashed potato. Grilled, buttered trout may be lightly sprinkled with salt, freshly ground pepper, and a dusting of mace, all that this delicately flavoured fish needs.

FISH SUPRÊME

This dish may be made the day before and kept in the refrigerator, removing it an hour before it is ready to go in the oven.

Cover 2 lb. raw fish (leatherjacket or your favourite fish) with water, add a little salt and a bay leaf, and simmer until the fish is cooked. Drain, reserving the liquid. Flake the fish while it is still hot, removing all bones, and put into an ovenproof dish.

Make Sauce Suprême as follows: Melt ¼ lb. butter or margarine, blend in ½ cup plain flour, and gradually add 1½ pints fish stock, stirring constantly until it thickens. Combine 4 eggs, ¼ pint thick cream, 2 tablespoons white wine, ½ teaspoon ground mace (or 1 teaspoon ground nutmeg) in a bowl, pour in some of the hot mixture, season with salt and pepper, mix well, then return all to the remaining contents of the saucepan. Stir gently over low heat for a moment only.

Pour the sauce over the fish, and top with soft white breadcrumbs which have been tossed in melted butter. Bake in a slow oven (about 300°F.) until heated through. **Serve hot with rice and chilled white wine.**

SAVOURY WELSH RAREBIT

3 tablespoons butter or
    margarine
4 tablespoons plain flour
1 teaspoon mustard
1 cup milk

2 teaspoons beef extract
    (mixed into ½ cup hot
    water)
½ lb. grated Cheddar cheese
Salt and pepper
Ground nutmeg

This cheese rarebit goes a long way.

Melt the butter, stir in the flour and mustard, slowly pour the milk in, then add the diluted beef extract. Add the cheese, season with salt and pepper, and cook, stirring until the mixture is smooth. Serve hot on buttered toast, topped with nutmeg.

AVOCADO SOUP

The most ambrosial soup I know. Ground or grated nutmeg sprinkled on each serving helps to minimize the richness without spoiling the bland texture.

1½ pints chicken broth (may
    be made with cubes)
2 large ripe avocado pears
½ pint cream

Extra cream
Ground nutmeg
Salt and pepper

Peel and stone the avocadoes, mash them, and put them into the chicken broth. Heat, then stir in ½ pint cream. Put the mixture through a sieve to remove any lumps, then return it to the saucepan, adding salt and pepper to taste. Bring slowly to simmering point without allowing it to boil. Serve hot with a dessertspoon of cream and a sprinkling of nutmeg in each bowl.

PAPRIKA

Paprika comes from a red, sweet pepper that is native to Central America and cultivated today in different parts of Europe and the United States. It is dried, ground, and sometimes blended with other peppers of the same family that differ in degrees of pungency. The best paprika is now said to come from Hungary.

The colour of paprika should be a rich, bright red, and the aroma warm and sweet. A splendid spice to use for flavouring, it is quite often regarded as a garnish only. Paprika gives Hungarian goulash its characteristic colour and taste; it is also valuable as a flavouring for delicately textured food such as crab, fish, chicken, cream sauces, eggs, and cheese dishes. It may be mixed into rice dishes and shaken onto split, baked potatoes, hors-d'œuvre, crumbed casseroles, or salads.

WALDORF SALAD

Paprika gives sparkle and relish to this salad, which is crisp with celery, apples, and nuts, glistens with orange cubes, and is folded together with a creamy sauce. It makes a pleasant change from a tossed green salad to serve with a main course.

> 1 *crisp eating apple, chopped*
> 1 *cup diced celery*
> 1 *large sweet orange, peeled and chopped*
> 1 *packet shelled, halved walnuts*
> *Paprika*

1 cup cream
1 tablespoon lemon juice
1 tablespoon sugar
½ teaspoon dry mustard
Salt and pepper

To make the sauce, stir the lemon juice, sugar, and mustard, with a little salt and pepper, into the cream, and beat till thick. Mix together the apple, celery, orange, and nuts and pour the sauce over. Toss well, then chill in the refrigerator. When ready to serve, turn onto a bed of lettuce, or onto leaves of fresh herbs, and sprinkle rosily with the paprika.

TEN-MINUTE CRAB PAPRIKA

This is an excellent entrée and makes a pleasant snack for a late supper.

Open a 6½-oz. tin of crab and flake it, removing all the sharp pieces. Have ready 1 pint of rich white sauce. Heat (do not boil), stirring in an egg which has been beaten with 1 dessertspoon paprika. In a separate saucepan warm 2 tablespoons brandy, set alight and carefully add to the sauce. Stir well, then add the crab. Pour into a buttered ovenproof dish or buttered scallop-shells, and top with breadcrumbs which have been tossed in melted butter. Brown in the oven. Serve with thin slices of lemon and very small squares of brown bread-and-butter.

HUNGARIAN VEAL GOULASH

2 lb. veal steak
2 onions, sliced
1 tablespoon shortening
1 tablespoon paprika
1 cup stock (may be made with a beef cube)

1 bay leaf
1 dessertspoon lemon juice
1 cup cream
1 tablespoon plain flour
Salt and pepper

Cut the veal into 2-inch cubes. Soften the onion in the shortening, add the meat, and brown all over. Add the paprika, and salt and pepper to taste, and cook a little longer. Add the stock, put in the bay leaf, cover the saucepan, and simmer for 1 hour, stirring occasionally. (Add a little more liquid if becoming too dry.) Pour the lemon juice into the cream, blend in the flour, add to the veal, and stir until thickened. Serve hot with poppy-seed noodles.

PEPPER

Black pepper and white pepper are both produced from the same climbing vine, which is native to the East Indies and cultivated in India, Sumatra, and Java. Pepper has been a valued spice for many hundreds of years; in the Middle Ages it was prized nearly as highly as gold and silver.

For black pepper, the berries are first picked from the vine, and then dried, when they become dark in colour, wrinkled, and very hot.

For white pepper, which is the same fruit, the dark outer husk is removed, leaving the smooth, parchment-coloured core, milder in flavour than black pepper.

Both black pepper and white pepper come in several forms: ground to a powder, left whole, or sometimes coarsely ground and mixed with sweet red pepper, sugar, and spices to make a delicious seasoned pepper. It is interesting to make your own mixture: over a small dish grind black and white pepper together in a mill, into the powder put a little sugar, ground cinnamon, paprika, and a pinch of ginger. Use this as a garnish as well as for flavouring.

Whole pepper, or peppercorns, are becoming increasingly popular: they may be poured into a mill and freshly ground over food while it is being prepared, and the mill may be passed round at table as well. The flavour of newly ground pepper is more aromatic, and it is a matter of taste whether black or white pepper is used for this purpose. Sometimes a mixture of the two is preferred.

A few whole peppercorns should be dropped into soups, stews, and casseroles, or when boiling salted pork, mutton, or beef. They are used too when making pickles, spice vinegars, and sauces.

PICKLED ONIONS

One year a crop of white onions failed and we were given a quantity of pearly little vegetables that were too small to send to market. When pickled they were crisp and spicy. Here is the way to pickle them: Peel 1 quart of small white onions, strew 1 oz. salt over them, and leave overnight. Next day, boil 1 quart of cider vinegar with 1 dessertspoon each of black peppercorns and whole cloves for 10 minutes. Wash the salt off the onions, shake dry in a colander, and add to the vinegar. Boil for 5 minutes. Remove the onions and pack into small jars or a large pickle jar, then pour the vinegar onto them. Seal the jars when the contents are cold.

SPICED VINEGAR

Empty 1 bottle of white wine or cider vinegar into a saucepan. Add 1 teaspoon each of peppercorns, whole cloves, ground ginger, and celery seed, also 1 cinnamon stick, 1 dried chili, and 1 dessertspoon sugar. Bring to the boil and simmer for 3 minutes. Cool and bottle without straining.

SAUSAGES AND LENTILS

2 lb. beef sausages	½ teaspoon peppercorns
2 medium-sized onions	2 tablespoons red lentils
1 clove of garlic	Salt
3 cloves	Plain flour
1 bay leaf	

Roll the sausages in plain flour, and peel and slice the onions and garlic. Put the ingredients in layers in an oven-proof dish and cover with water. With the lid on, bake in a slow oven (275° to 300°F.) for 2½ hours.

SAFFRON

Saffron comes from the orange-coloured stigmas of a mauve-flowering crocus, native to Asia and parts of Europe. It is a rare and expensive spice because only the hand-picked stigmas are used and it requires over 200,000 of these to make one pound: fortunately only a small quantity is needed to colour and flavour food.

Saffron has been prized from the most ancient times for use in food, medicine, and dyes; in *The Bible as History* we are told that the colourful garments of the Children of Israel owed their brightness to nature: saffron for yellow, madder-root for red, and the murex snail supplied purple.

Culpeper describes saffron as being a herb of the sun, and says: "It refreshes the spirits, and is good against fainting-fits and the palpitation of the heart." But he cautions against an immoderate amount being taken. Sir Francis Bacon thought so highly of this herb that he said: "What made the English people sprightly was the liberal use of saffron in their broths and sweet-meats." (Eleanour Sinclair Rohde, *A Garden of Herbs*.) In medieval days saffron was also popular as a dye for the hair.

There is a town in England called Saffron Walden where this crocus was grown extensively; the arms of the town have three saffron flowers pictured within turreted walls. Saffron Hill, now a London thoroughfare, was once part of the gardens of Ely Place where quantities of saffron were grown.

The warmly bitter aroma and the gold colour of saffron

give certain dishes their traditional flavour and colour: the saffron cakes of Cornwall are well known; saffron is an important ingredient in the classic French fish soup Bouillabaisse, in Arroz con Pollo (Rice with Chicken), and in Paella; it also enhances some sauces, breads, cakes, fish, chicken, and rice dishes.

Today saffron comes from different parts of the world and is almost as precious as gold dust; when ground to a russet powder it is packaged carefully in envelopes; it is also available in whole orange and gold threads. When using the threads, crush the required number and infuse in the hot milk or other liquid which the recipe calls for. The powder may be infused in liquid or sifted with flour.

SAFFRON BUNS

An old recipe from an authority on English folk cookery, Florence White, who includes it in her collection, *Good English Food*.

Take 3½ lb. flour, ½ lb. butter, ½ pint cream of milk; set the milk on the fire, put in the butter and a good deal of sugar, strain saffron to your taste into the milk, take three or four eggs, with one yolk and one ounce of compressed yeast, put the milk to it when almost cold, with salt, and coriander seeds; knead them all together, make them up into small cakes, or buns, set them to rise and bake them in a quick oven.

To prepare the saffron take half a drachm and cut very fine with scissors, pour over half a cup of boiling water and steep overnight.

SAFFRON RISOTTO

A delicately flavoured golden dish to serve with fricasseed chicken, fish, or a veal casserole. This method of cooking a risotto is recommended provided the cooking time is watched and the quantities given are measured accurately.

2 *oz. butter*	1 *cup rice*
1 *medium-sized onion, chopped*	1 *pint chicken broth (may be made with chicken cubes)*
1 *clove of garlic, chopped*	
1 *small green capsicum, chopped*	¼ *teaspoon saffron*

Infuse the saffron, whether ground or whole, in the hot
chicken broth. Melt the butter in a fireproof pan or casserole,
add the onion, garlic, and capsicum, then the rice, turning
until the grains are shining and coated. Add the saffron-
flavoured chicken broth. Bring to the boil, put the lid on, and
place in a moderate oven (350°F.) to bake for 30 minutes.

SUNNY SAFFRON DUMPLINGS

1 *cup self-raising flour*	*¼ cup milk*
A pinch of salt	*A pinch of powdered*
2 oz. butter	*saffron*
2 teaspoons dried parsley	

These dumplings are for a meat or chicken casserole.

Sift the flour and salt into a bowl, rub in the butter, and
add the parsley. Heat the milk and saffron together, add to
the flour, and mix to a firm dough. Pat out on a floured
surface, and roll lightly. Mark deep incisions in the form of
squares with a knife, slide in one piece onto the cooked,
bubbling casserole, replace the lid, and cook for 20 minutes.
Serve immediately.

BOUILLABAISSE

It is said that only in France may one taste real bouillabaisse, for the original recipe calls for several different kinds
of fish that are not available in other countries. Nevertheless,
there are many versions of this popular fish soup, and this
one has a delicious and unusual flavour and aroma, is quite
inexpensive, and is quickly prepared even by the busiest
cook.

4 *lb. boned, filleted fish*	*2 cloves of garlic, cut very*
cut into pieces	*fine*
½ cup vegetable oil	*1 teaspoon saffron*
4 *tomatoes, peeled and*	*1 wine-glass white wine*
chopped	*½ teaspoon thyme*
3 *onions, peeled and*	*Freshly ground pepper*
chopped	*1 teaspoon salt*

Trout is excellent if available.

Heat the oil in a large casserole, and fry in it the tomato, onion, garlic, and saffron, together with salt and pepper. Add the sliced fish, wine, thyme, and bay leaf, cover with water (about 2 quarts), bring to the boil, and simmer for 10 minutes. Serve hot. Accompany with slices of a French loaf.

SAFFRON GOOSEBERRY SHORTCAKE

2 cups self-raising flour
¼ teaspoon powdered
  saffron
¼ teaspoon salt
½ cup brown sugar
¼ lb. butter or margarine

2 eggs, beaten
½ cup milk
One 1-lb. tin gooseberries
1 dessertspoon arrowroot,
  blended with a little milk

This is a refreshing sweet in summer. It may be eaten for afternoon tea if you wish.

Sift the flour, saffron, and salt into a bowl, add the brown sugar, rub in the butter, and add the eggs and milk. Spoon into a greased, lightly floured 8-inch recessed tin and bake in a hot oven (400°F.) for 15 minutes. Cool and turn onto a cake rack. Open the tin of gooseberries, drain the liquid into a saucepan and simmer it until it is reduced a little. Thicken it with the blended arrowroot, stir in the gooseberries, cool, and pour onto the shortcake. Serve with thick cream.

If fresh gooseberries are used, stew the fruit in the usual way, thickening the syrup with arrowroot when cooked.

SALT

Salt is included here because it is essential in all types of cooking. Its value as an antiseptic and its use in medicine are well known.

Salt, or sodium chloride, occurs naturally in sea water; mineral deposits of rock salt are the crystalline evidence of vast salt lakes and seas long since vanished from the earth's surface. Smaller quantities are found near hot springs and mineral waters, the salt from the solution being precipitated and occurring in layers.

Refined free-running table salt (which has magnesium carbonate added to prevent it from caking) is seen on every grocer's shelf, as well as a coarser quality known as common salt. Some table salt has a proportion of iodine added to it as a preventive against goitre. Salt crystals for grinding over food should be put into a wooden salt mill as a companion to the pepper mill. The crystals are obtainable from some butchers' shops and delicatessens.

There are many seasoned salts which have gone through a process to capture the flavour required; some popular flavours at present are celery salt, garlic salt, mushroom salt, parsley salt, salt seasoned with spices and herbs, and health salt containing dehydrated vegetables and herbs. There is a hickory-smoked salt smelling of wood smoke, which is particularly attractive to people living in the depths of big cities miles from forests and open country.

A seasoned salt for the kitchen, barbecues, or the table

is very useful: an interesting blend is easily made by a selection from the spice shelf. A pestle-and-mortar for grinding and pounding the ingredients together is needed, and whether it is made from marble or smooth wood it is a practical and handsome kitchen implement.

SEASONED SALT

Grind together in a mortar 1 teaspoon celery seed and 1 teaspoon dried rosemary. Add 1 teaspoon each of ground mace and paprika, ½ teaspoon sugar, and 1 tablespoon table salt. Put in a small airtight bottle and use as required.

MONOSODIUM GLUTAMATE

Monosodium glutamate, or MSG, is mentioned as an ingredient in many recipes. Its purpose is to enhance and bring out, or to restore, the characteristic flavour of food, not to impart an aroma of its own. It is made from crystals produced from vegetable protein, and has various trade names, its description being "essence of taste".

166

Red Cabbage Casserole
with Pork Sausages
(p.174) with Mulled Ale
(p.175).

TURMERIC

Turmeric is a perennial plant of the ginger family, native to India and parts of Asia. The dried, aromatic root is ground to a brilliant yellow powder which gives a commercial curry blend its typical colour and much of its flavour; it is used in the East as a dye for cottons and silks as well as for flavouring food.

The vivid hue and pungent scent of this spice seems essentially Eastern in character: "What is the scent of a Bazaar? Who can say? . . . Taking it as a whole, however, I fancy the smell of turmeric brings back more than anything else the wonderful kaleidoscope of colours in an Indian bazaar." (*India*, by Mortimer Menpes.)

The mellow fragrance and bright colour of turmeric has made it popular as an ingredient in pickles and chutneys, and in mustard-powder blends. A small amount may be used for colouring cakes, and it is excellent in rice dishes; turmeric is often added to fish kedgeree, devilled eggs, French dressings, and fish stews; a pinch stirred into a smooth white sauce gives colour and an elusive, rather peppery, taste.

FRENCH DRESSING

Take 1 tablespoon of lemon juice or white vinegar and blend in 2 tablespoons of vegetable oil, some freshly ground pepper, a little salt, a pinch of sugar, and a few grains of mustard powder. Prepare well in advance and keep in a small screw-top jar or covered jug until the last moment, before the

*Steak Kebabs (p. 75) with
Lemon and Mustard Seed
Chutney (p.198).*

salad is tossed, when the mixture should be thoroughly stirred or vigorously shaken.

This dressing is also used as a marinade. One teaspoon of turmeric added to the mixture with the mustard is delicious for a change, either when tossing a salad or for marinades.

TROPICAL POTATO SALAD

3 *cups diced cooked potatoes*	*A little lemon juice*
1 *cup banana circles*	2 *teaspoons turmeric*
1 *cup finely chopped shallots (include the green part)*	1 *cup mayonnaise*
	2 *hard-boiled eggs, sliced*
	Salt and pepper

This salad has a pleasant and subtle combination of flavours.

Sprinkle lemon juice over the banana circles to prevent discoloration. While the potatoes are still warm, season them with salt and pepper and add the banana and shallot. Blend the turmeric with the mayonnaise and mix gently through the salad. Add the egg slices last. Chill before serving.

KEDGEREE

This is a good luncheon or breakfast dish, which may be prepared the night before it is needed.

1 *cup cooked rice*	1 *capsicum, chopped*
1 *lb. any one of the following: smoked and flaked cooked cod, tinned salmon or tuna, prawns or lobster*	2 *cloves of garlic, chopped*
	2 *teaspoons turmeric*
	Juice of a lemon
	½ *teaspoon ground ginger*
	Salt and pepper
¼ *lb. butter or margarine*	2 *hard-boiled eggs, shelled*
1 *onion, peeled and chopped*	1 *teaspoon dried parsley*

Melt butter and soften onion, capsicum, and garlic in it. Add turmeric, lemon juice, ginger, and a little salt and pepper. Lightly stir in fish and rice, and when thoroughly mixed together turn into a dish and heat in the oven before serving. Garnish with eggs cut into circles, and with parsley.

AROMATIC SEEDS

ANISEED

Anise is a sun-loving annual plant, native to Middle Eastern countries. The clusters of white flowers are followed by small oval seeds which are light brown in colour and taste warmly of licorice. Anise was known many thousands of years ago: it is referred to in the Bible and, as I mentioned at the beginning of this book, the Romans ate cakes made with these digestion-aiding seeds to conclude their enormous feasts. Helen Noyes Webster quotes from Grieve and Leyel: "It was used in a spiced cake at the end of a meal by the Romans in Virgil's time to prevent indigestion; a cake which was brought in at the end of a marriage feast, it is perhaps the origin of today's spicy wedding cake."

Anise is used extensively in cooking, in medicine for digestive complaints, and as an ingredient in the liqueur Anisette. It is grown mainly for the seeds, although the leaves may be used in salads and as a garnish. Aniseed flavours breads, rolls, cakes, biscuits, and sweet pastry for fruit pies and tarts. It may also be used in cheeses, in milk beverages and puddings, and when cooking vegetables such as carrots and cabbage, when little or no water is used.

With some of the other fragrant seeds, aniseed may be pressed into butter to be spread on top of "brown-and-serve" rolls before they are put into the oven. Line a rustic basket with a table napkin and fill it with hot rolls, some topped with aniseed, others with sesame seed, poppy

173

seed, dill seed, celery seed, or caraway seed. If you have herbs growing, garnish with leaves of anise, burnet, or dill. These rolls are excellent to serve with a main dish for luncheon or supper, the seeds giving them a delicious flavour and crunchiness.

ANISE COOKIES

4 oz. butter or margarine	A pinch of salt
1 cup raw sugar	1 cup rolled oats
1 egg	1½ cups desiccated coconut
4 oz. self-raising flour	2 teaspoons aniseed

Cream the butter and sugar, add the egg and beat well. Stir in the sifted flour and salt, and add the rolled oats, coconut, and aniseed, mixing well together to a stiff consistency. Roll into small balls between the hands, put on a greased oven tray, and bake in a moderate oven (350° to 375°F.) for 12 to 15 minutes. Cool on the tray before storing.

RED CABBAGE CASSEROLE WITH PORK SAUSAGES

Aniseed gives its quota to the other delicious smells which help to make this a fragrant winter dish for six hungry people. Serve it at supper-time with baked-jacket potatoes, and with mulled ale (see next recipe).

1 red cabbage	¼ pint strong chicken stock
3 onions, peeled and	(made with 1 cube)
chopped	1 teaspoon black pepper-
3 green apples, chopped	corns
with the skin on	½ teaspoon salt
3 tablespoons raw or brown	1 dessertspoon aniseed
sugar	2 lb. pork sausages
2 tablespoons cider	½ lb. bacon
vinegar	

Shred the cabbage and put it into a large casserole with the onion, apple, sugar, vinegar, chicken stock, peppercorns, salt, and aniseed. Mix well, put the lid on, and bake in a slow oven (300°F.) for 3 hours, putting scrubbed potatoes into the oven for the last 1½ hours. Towards the end of the cooking time, fry the sausages and bacon, turning them until browned and cooked. Put them into the cabbage mixture before serving with the baked potatoes.

MULLED ALE

This recipe is from *Mrs Beeton's Book of Household Management.*

1 *quart good ale*	*A pinch of grated nutmeg*
1 *glass rum or brandy*	*A good pinch of ground*
1 *tablespoon castor sugar*	*ginger*
A pinch of ground cloves	

Put the ale, sugar, cloves, nutmeg, and ginger into an ale warmer or stewpan, and bring nearly to boiling point. Add the brandy, and more sugar and flavouring if necessary, and serve at once.

ANISEED CARROTS

Cut carrots into straws, put them in a saucepan with 2 tablespoons water, 1 tablespoon raw or brown sugar, 1 oz. butter, and 1 teaspoon aniseed, adding some salt and pepper. Put the lid on and simmer gently for 10 to 15 minutes, when they will be cooked yet crisp and slightly candied.

CARAWAY SEED

Caraway is a biennial plant, native to the Mediterranean shores and now indigenous all over Europe. It is grown largely for the aromatic seeds, but the roots are also edible, being boiled and eaten like carrots. The German name for caraway is *kummel*, the well-known liqueur of this name having oil of caraway in its composition.

Caraway seed is very good for the digestion, and is the reason why it is traditionally included in, or eaten with, certain food. Florence White explains this very clearly in *Good English Food*:

"Roasted apples eaten with caraway comfits are a homely early eighteenth-century preventative of many of the ills that flesh is heir to.

"An old gentleman of over eighty wrote in 1714 that he had eaten a roasted apple with caraway comfits every night for fifty years, and had never suffered from constipation, gout, or stone or any other distemper incident to old age.

"The custom is a much older one, dating back to the time of ancient Greece and Rome, and is probably the origin of the old saying: 'An apple a day keeps the doctor away.'

"Apples are apt to cause flatulence, for which caraway seeds and comfits give relief, and it was the custom of our ancestors to serve a dish of baked apples and caraway comfits after a meal."

There are many other virtues attributed to caraway: it

was put into love potions; and Dioscorides, the great Greek physician who lived in the first century A.D., prescribed it for "girls of pale face".

Caraway seed is used in breads, particularly rye. Certain cheeses are flavoured with caraway, and it is the ingredient which gives seed cake its name. Caraway seed also flavours pickles, soups, vegetables, and meat and fish dishes.

CARAWAY RICE RING AND TUNA

A tasty meal for meatless days. The moulded rice looks colourful and attractive.

One 15-oz. tin tuna	1 pint milk
2 oz. butter or margarine, and 2 extra tablespoons	2 cups, or 1 lb., rice
	1 dessertspoon caraway seed
1 heaped tablespoon plain flour	2 oz. red caviar
	1½ teaspoons dried parsley
1 dessertspoon paprika	Salt and pepper

Melt 2 oz. butter in a saucepan, blend in the flour and paprika, and mix to a paste. Gradually add the milk, season with salt and pepper, and add the tuna. Keep hot.

Put the rice into a quantity of boiling salted water, and when cooked drain it in a colander, running some hot water over it to separate the grains. Shake well, turn into a bowl, fold in extra butter (melted), also caraway seeds, caviar, and parsley. Turn into a ring mould, press the rice in firmly, then unmould immediately onto a large platter. Pour some of the hot tuna into the centre of the ring, and the rest around it. Serve at once.

PINEAPPLE AND CHEESE IN THE SHELL

Cut a large ripe pineapple cleanly in half lengthwise through the green top, and scoop out the flesh, discarding the core. Chop the flesh into cubes, put into a bowl, and add 1 cup sugar and 1 tablespoon of sherry. Cover and leave for an hour or so. Chop ½ lb. mild Cheddar cheese into cubes and add to the pineapple, then stir in 1 tablespoon of caraway seed. Spoon the mixture into the pineapple shells, and chill.

SEED SPONGE CAKE

Seed cakes were made in some parts of England at least four hundred years ago, at the end of the wheat-sowing season.

3 eggs, separated
5 oz. castor sugar
1 cup self-raising flour
1½ tablespoons cornflour
1 dessertspoon butter

1 tablespoon orange-flower water (from the pharmacist)
2 tablespoons water
1 tablespoon caraway seed
A pinch of salt

Beat the egg whites until stiff and dry, and make a stiff meringue by gradually adding the sugar and beating until the grains are dissolved. Gently mix in the egg yolks. Sift the flour, salt, and cornflour together three times and fold this lightly into the egg and sugar mixture. Heat together the butter, orange-flower water, and water, and fold it into the flour mixture at once together with the caraway seed. Pour into a well-greased and floured tin, sprinkle the top with castor sugar, and bake in a moderately hot oven (400°F.) for 20 minutes.

CARDAMOM SEED

Cardamom is a perennial plant originating from India. It is valued for the small irregularly shaped seeds which have a strong, cool, eucalyptus-scented flavour. Cardamom is an ingredient in Indian curry powder blends, and in other forms of Indian cooking. It is also popular in Scandinavian cookery.

A delicious Indian pudding was prepared for us one day from some quite ordinary ingredients combined with exotic ones to give an exquisite appearance and distinctive flavour. It was simply a rice pudding called *Kheer*; the milk, rice, and sugar were soaked together, then cooked in a double saucepan with a grated carrot. When the rice was cooked, cracked cardamom seed was added, the rice mixture was put into a glass dish and covered with gossamer-thin sheets of pure silver, then finished with a pattern of shelled almonds shaved thinly. It was eaten cold, and the taste was cool and aromatic: a sensible dessert to eat in a hot country and probably following a spicy curry dish. The silver seemed to melt in the mouth, and in fact when a tissue-wrapped bundle of silver sheets was produced to demonstrate the fine texture, on handling, it was so ephemeral that it appeared to float away. Only gentle and practised fingers could succeed in creating the finished effect we saw. In India, gold leaf is used as well for puddings on special occasions.

Cardamom seed is very hard and needs to be cracked by pressing the required amount with a rolling pin before using it. Blend it into the curry powder, or put a teaspoon into a pastry mixture before adding the liquid; use it in gingerbread, in coffee cake, in fruit dishes, and in rice pudding. Crush a few seeds and put them in a small bowl to be handed with coffee crystals for black coffee.

BAKED PEARS AND CARDAMOM

When fruit is baked in the oven, especially in wine or in a liqueur, it has a better flavour than when cooked on top of the stove.

Peel, slice, and core pears, lay them in a shallow ovenproof dish, sprinkle with sugar, and add 2 tablespoons wine or liqueur. (A Tia Maria which has a chocolate flavour was used successfully on one occasion.) Sprinkle with 2 teaspoons of cracked cardamom seed. Bake in a moderate oven (350°F.) until the pears are soft. Allow to cool. Serve with a little thick cream: the flavour of this dish must not be lost by drowning it with too much cream or custard.

CARDAMOM HONEY DRESSING

A delicious and nourishing dressing for fruit salad, halved melons, waffles, or corn cakes.

Beat ½ pint clear honey in an electric mixer until it is light in colour. Gradually add 2 tablespoons lemon juice and a few drops of orange-flower water. Stir in ½ teaspoon cracked cardamom seed. Keep in a screw-top glass jar.

ICED BEETROOT AND CARDAMOM SALAD

This method of cooking beetroots seems to preserve the goodness and flavour, and as Mrs Beeton observes, without "loss of their beautiful colour".

Place 4 large beets in a dish and bake in a slow oven for about 3 hours. Cool slightly, peel and slice thinly. Sprinkle with sugar, a little salt, and 2 teaspoons cracked cardamom seed. Pour French dressing (page 88) over, and chill thoroughly.

CELERY SEED

Celery seed is the dried fruit of the celery plant, thought to be native to Europe. However, it is said that originally it was the pot-herb known as smallage, which is wild celery: indeed, many of today's cultivated vegetables were once the simple pot-herbs of our forbears. Culpeper describes smallage in his *Complete Herbal* thus: "The roots are about a finger thick, wrinkled, and sinking deep in the earth, of a white colour, from which spring many winged leaves of a yellow colour . . . the roots, leaves, and seed are used."

Mrs C. F. Leyel says that celery juice "is an anti-acid tonic and stimulant rich in volatile oils and fruit sugar. It is a simple and effective remedy for some rheumatic complaints." It is interesting to read from quite another source that celery has the property to help rheumatism. Here is a recipe from *Lotions and Potions*: "Boil 1 oz. of celery seed in 1 pint of water until reduced to half. Strain, bottle and cork carefully. Take 1 teaspoonful twice a day in a little water for a fortnight. Repeat again if required."

Celery seed is small and brownish, and has a potent taste. It is probably one of the most popular flavourings on the spice shelf. It goes into tomato juice and seafood cocktails; in pickles and chutney; on top of breads and rolls; in soups, stews, fish dishes, and nearly all vegetable dishes; in white sauces and mayonnaise; and in cheese and herb-butter mixtures. Commercial celery salt is flavoured with ground celery seed, or with ground dried celery stems.

CABBAGE ASPIC

4 *cups finely shredded*	1 *cup sugar*
cabbage	4 *cups cold water*
2 *cups chopped celery*	2 *cups very hot water*
1 *red capsicum, thinly sliced*	1 *cup cider vinegar*
1 *tablespoon celery seed*	*Salt*
4 *tablespoons gelatine*	*Freshly ground pepper*

Green and glistening, this salad is a crisp and delicious accompaniment to a main meat course.

Pour the 2 cups of very hot water (just off the boil) onto the gelatine and sugar, and stir until both are dissolved. Add the 4 cups of cold water and the vinegar, and leave until cool, but not set. Stir in the rest of the ingredients, and pour into a rinsed-out mould. When set, unmould onto a bed of fresh herbs or lettuce leaves.

SHARP MAYONNAISE

To be eaten with cold meat.

Mix together 1 cup mayonnaise, ¼ cup prepared horse-radish, and 2 teaspoons of celery seed.

AROMATIC SWEET POTATOES

Peel and slice 1 lb. sweet potatoes and arrange in a buttered ovenproof dish. Top with slices of rindless bacon and halved pineapple rings, and sprinkle with brown sugar, freshly ground pepper, and 2 teaspoons celery seed. Bake in a moderate oven (350°F.) for 40 or 45 minutes. Serve with meat casserole, grills, or baked veal.

CORIANDER SEED

Coriander is an annual with pink-tinged, delicately lacy flowers. It is native to southern Europe and the Near East and grows to 2 feet in height. It is one of the oldest herbs known to man. In the Bible the seed is likened to manna, tasting ". . . like wafers made with honey". Today it is grown in many parts of the world.

Coriander was said by many of the early herbalists to associate well with chervil and dill, which blossom at the same time; this suggestion is also probably intended to carry out the interesting theory that certain plants are sympathetic to each other, one strengthening the other with special properties, perhaps by giving off an odour unpleasant to insects which would otherwise attack the vulnerable plant growing next to it; in return, this plant would contain qualities lacking in the other.

Coriander seeds are small, slightly oval, and bleached-looking, with an agreeable spicy flavour. Unfortunately the seed is susceptible to weevils and is therefore not easy to obtain; perhaps the best way of having it is to grow it oneself. As the seeds have the power of remaining fertile for up to five years, there is no need to worry over fresh supplies for planting. When the flowers have fallen, collect the ripe seed and store in an airtight jar: the fragrance improves with keeping.

Coriander seed is an ingredient in curry blends; it is popular in some Spanish food and in many Eastern dishes; it flavours cheese, breads, rolls, cakes, and pastries and is frequently used in sausages, preserves, and confections.

ARABIAN STUFFED CAPSICUMS

12 medium-sized green
  capsicums
2 cups stock (may be made
  with 2 soup cubes)
2 cups cooked, chopped
  lamb, or 1 lb. minced steak
2 cups cooked rice
2 tablespoons skinned,
  slivered almonds

2 onions, chopped
2 teaspoons crushed
  coriander seed
½ teaspoon ground
  cinnamon
2 tomatoes, peeled and diced
1 tablespoon chopped
  olives
Salt and pepper

Prepare the capsicums for stuffing by removing a piece from the top of each and scooping out the seeds. Mix together the lamb, rice, onion, almonds, coriander seed, cinnamon, tomato, and olives, seasoning with a little salt and pepper. Stuff the capsicums, place in a baking dish, replace capsicum tops, cover with the stock, and bake in a moderate oven (350°F.) for 1 hour, basting frequently. If any meat mixture is left over, form it into balls and put them in the dish too.

CORIANDER APPLE CRUMBLE

Cover the bottom of a buttered shallow ovenproof dish with peeled, sliced cooking apples, sprinkle with 1 tablespoon raw sugar and 1 teaspoon ground cinnamon. In a bowl rub together until crumbly 1 cup plain flour, ½ cup raw sugar, and ¼ lb. butter. Press and smooth this on top of the apples, then sprinkle with crushed coriander seed (try 1 teaspoon to begin with, and increase the amount next time you make this dessert, if you wish). Bake in a moderate oven (350°F.) for about 30 minutes. Serve hot or cold with cream.

CORIANDER HONEY CAKES

1 lb. honey
¼ lb. butter
1 lb. plain flour
4 tablespoons milk

1 teaspoon carbonate of
  soda
2 teaspoons crushed
  coriander seed

Put the honey and butter together in a saucepan and heat till bubbling. Cool a little, and pour into a bowl. Sift the flour and soda into the honey mixture, add the milk, then the crushed coriander seed. Chill, then turn onto a floured surface, form into cakes, and bake on greased and floured trays in a moderately hot oven (400°F.) for 15 minutes. Allow to cool on trays. Store in containers.

CUMIN SEED

Cumin is a small annual sun-loving herb, native to Egypt. The pale-pink flowers are followed by parchment-coloured seeds, the flavour of which almost holds the key to the pungent taste of curry powder. Some say that this seed resembles caraway in flavour; the seeds of both are very aromatic, but to my mind so essentially different that one could not easily replace the other. Cumin is mentioned in the Bible, the seed having been valued for the digestion, as well as for culinary purposes, for many centuries.

Cumin seed is used mainly in the blending of curry powder, chili powder, and in flavouring dishes from the Near and Middle East. A teaspoon or two of the mildly hot seed gives an Eastern flavour to food: it is often used in rye bread; in pickles and chutney; in rice, cabbage, and bean dishes; in meat dishes; and to mash into cottage cheese with a little lemon juice for a spread or dip.

TURKISH CUCUMBERS

4 cucumbers	1 teaspoon salt
1 carton yoghurt	1 tablespoon white vinegar
1 clove of garlic, finely chopped	1 teaspoon cumin seed
	1 teaspoon chopped mint

Soak the garlic, salt, and vinegar together. Strain. Peel the cucumbers and slice them thinly lengthwise. Put the yoghurt in a bowl and stir in gradually the strained vinegar. Add the cumin seed. Pour the dressing over the cucumbers, sprinkle with mint, and serve slightly chilled.

LAMB SHANKS ARMENIAN

6 *lamb shanks*
2 *tablespoons plain flour*
2 *cloves of garlic, finely chopped*
1 *onion, chopped*
1 *capsicum, chopped*
2 *teaspoons cumin seed*

1 *teaspoon black peppercorns*
1 *tablespoon lemon juice*
1 *dill cucumber, sliced*
3 *cups tomato juice*
Salt

Roll the shanks in the flour and place in a large casserole with the other ingredients. Put the lid on, and bake in a slow oven (275° to 300°F.) for 2½ hours. Serve hot with brown rice and plenty of the savoury liquid.

CUMIN AND ROSE GERANIUM DROPS

6 *oz. butter*
1 *cup sugar*
2 *eggs*
3 *cups self-raising flour*
2 *teaspoons cumin seed*

Rose geranium jelly
(page 48) or other
preserve
A pinch of salt

To make these fragrant confections, cream the butter and sugar, beat in the eggs one at a time, fold in the sifted flour and salt, and add the cumin seed. Form into small balls with the hands, roll in sugar, make a depression in the centre of each, and fill with rose geranium jelly. Bake in a moderate oven (375°F.). Cool on a tray and store in an air-tight container.

DILL SEED

Dill is an annual plant, a native of southern Europe. Many centuries ago it found its way, like numerous other herbs, to the colder parts of Europe, where it became an attractive and useful wayside "weed". Today it grows in countries all over the world. The name stems from the Norse word *dilla*, meaning to lull: dill water, a decoction made from the seeds, was given to babies to soothe them in those far-off days, just as it is today. Yellow-flowering dill, very like fennel in appearance, is grown for its fresh, fern-like leaves and for the aromatic buff-coloured seeds which give food added flavour and make it more easily assimilated. It is more than coincidence that dill is put with cucumbers in the making of dill pickles, for this vegetable has the reputation of being rather indigestible. It is also one of the most appropriate herbs to use in cole slaw and in steamed cabbage. If caraway seed is not popular with some people, dill seed may be substituted, for the flavour though similar is not as strong as that of caraway.

According to a charming American leaflet about herbs, dill and fennel seed were known as "meetin' seed", having been given to children to eat during long Sunday sermons.

Dill seed is sprinkled on breads, rolls, and apple pie; it is used in sauces for vegetables and fish; it goes into stews and soups; in the pot with those vegetables which need the minimum of water during cooking, such as shredded cabbage and finely sliced chokoes; it flavours pickles, chutney, potato salad, and sauerkraut; and is often cooked with veal, pork, and kidneys.

DILL SAUCE

1½ cups white sauce
1 tablespoon sherry

1 medium-sized dill
  cucumber, diced
2 teaspoons dill seed

To be eaten with any fried fish.

Mix the sherry into the hot white sauce, blend well, and add the cucumber and dill seed. Serve hot.

DILL-CHEESE DIP OR SPREAD

One 4-oz. packet of cream
  cheese
2 tablespoons thin cream
2 teaspoons dill seed

2 teaspoons lemon juice
1 tablespoon grated onion
Salt and pepper

Blend the cheese and cream together, then add the rest of the ingredients, and mix well.

HOT SLAW

4 cups finely shredded
  cabbage
2 eggs
¼ cup water
2 tablespoons lemon juice

1 tablespoon sugar
2 teaspoons dill seed
1 tablespoon butter or
  margarine
Salt and pepper

Break the eggs into a saucepan and whisk with a wire whisk. Add the water, lemon juice, sugar, and dill seed, season with a little salt and pepper, and whisk well again. Place on a low flame, add the butter, and stir with a wooden spoon until the mixture thickens. Stir in the cabbage, coating thoroughly with the dressing. Serve hot.

FENNEL SEED

Fennel is another native from Mediterranean countries. Long ago it was taken to other lands by the Romans, and today it is widely grown in most parts of the world. The two best-known varieties are perennial fennel and the annual Florence fennel. The former kind grows tall and feathery, and in early autumn its massed golden flowers foam along country roadsides; the leaves are not as tender and delicately flavoured as those of the annual fennel, which is a lower-growing type with bulbous, edible stems, a little like a squat celery in appearance. Fennel seed comes from both of these kinds, but if you are growing your own, it is suggested that Florence fennel is the wiser choice, since all parts of the plant may be used. The broad white stems should be sliced thinly and added to green salads; they are crisp and nutty, and the flavour bears a strong resemblance to that of aniseed, as in fact do all parts of this herb. The leaves are traditionally an accompaniment to fish, either in a sauce, or to be cooked with it. When the plant has finished flowering, and the heads are heavy with seed, collect and store the seeds.

Fennel is mentioned in the early Anglo-Saxon herbals; it was regarded as one of nine sacred herbs, and its properties were said to have great physical benefits and to guard against unseen evil. One of its ancient uses was for the restoration of eyesight; another use was as a decoction "to make those more lean that are too fat".

Chaucer mentions fennel:

> *Downe by a little path I fond*
> *Of mintes full and fennell greene.*

Shakespeare too knew fennel well:

OPHELIA: There's fennel for you, and columbines; there's rue for you; and here's some for me; we may call it herb of grace o' Sundays.

Fennel is represented in Shakespeare's birthplace garden; the plant list is long and reads like poetry; amongst the medlars and mints grow bay trees, box, and briar; columbine, cuckoo-buds, elder, and fennel; savory, sedge, thyme, and many more.

Longfellow describes tall, perennial fennel in "The Goblet of Life":

> *Above the lowly plants it towers,*
> *The fennel, with its yellow flowers,*
> *And in an earlier age than ours*
> *Was gifted with the wondrous powers,*
> *Lost vision to restore.*

Today fennel is considered as a useful flavouring for food, and the seed goes into breads and cakes, on top of rolls and fruit tarts, and in cheese mixtures and spreads. It gives an aromatic taste to fish dishes, and also to meat dishes, especially pork, liver, and kidneys; it goes into pickles and sauces, and is an ingredient in some curry blends.

KIDNEYS AND MUSHROOMS

6 *sheep's kidneys*	1 *teaspoon paprika*
2 *oz. butter*	½ *pint stock (may be made*
1 *clove of garlic, chopped*	*with a soup-cube)*
1 *onion, chopped*	*One 8-oz. tin mushrooms*
1 *rounded tablespoon plain*	1 *scant dessertspoon fennel*
flour	*seed*
	Salt and pepper

Melt the butter in a heavy frying pan, and soften the garlic and onion in it. Skin the kidneys, slice them, and put them into the pan. Cook gently, turning them. Stir in the flour, allowing it to brown slightly, then add the paprika, stock, mushrooms, and fennel seed. Stir until the sauce has thickened, adding salt and pepper to taste. Serve hot with buttered toast.

FENNEL SEED POTATO CAKE

A new and tasty way with potatoes is always welcome. This dish is very little trouble to prepare. Peel and slice 1 lb. potatoes thinly, butter a baking dish and put in a layer of potatoes, 1 teaspoon fennel seed, and some salt and freshly ground pepper. Dot with butter. Repeat. Finish by pouring ¼ pint thin cream over the top. Bake in a moderate oven (350°F.) for about 1 hour. If becoming too crisp around the edges, cover with a piece of brown paper. Test with a fork: when soft in the centre, the potato cake is cooked. Serve hot.

FENNEL TEA

Boil ½ pint water with 1 teaspoon fennel seeds for 5 minutes. Strain.

JUNIPER BERRIES

These are the fruit of a small, evergreen tree, native to Europe, northern parts of Africa, and Arctic regions. The berries do not ripen until the second or third year, when they are picked and dried. While the berries are ripening from green to silvery purple, new small cones are forming on the tree at the same time.

The resinous, sweetly sharp flavour of juniper berries not only gives a delightful smell and taste to food, but an oil from the berries is used medicinally for the treatment of kidney and digestive complaints; the aromatic globes also provide the flavouring in the manufacture of gin.

In France, juniper berries are included in many stews, while in Germany they are considered an excellent addition to sauerkraut and cole slaw. These berries are almost essential with game dishes, such as duck, grouse, quail, hare, rabbit, and venison; they are equally delicious in a stuffing for the domestic fowl, duck, goose, or turkey. Six to nine berries are usually sufficient to give the desired flavour, and they should be crushed first with the back of a wooden spoon: this is easy to do because they are soft.

CHICKEN JUNIPER

This recipe allows 4 or 5 good servings. If you want enough for 6 to 8 people, cook two chickens and double the quantity of the ingredients.

Duck may be cooked in the same way, substituting the mixed herbs for sage in the stuffing.

193

One 2½- to 3-lb. chicken,
  cleaned and ready to cook
¾ cup soft breadcrumbs
2 teaspoons mixed herbs
9 to 12 juniper berries
Salt and pepper

A little grated lemon rind
½ pint white wine
2 carrots, thinly sliced
2 shallots, thinly sliced
1 tablespoon butter

Combine the breadcrumbs, mixed herbs, slightly crushed juniper berries, salt, pepper, and lemon rind, and stuff the chicken. Spread the butter over the chicken and place it in a baking dish. Pour in the white wine and add the carrot and shallot. Cover the chicken with foil and bake in a moderate oven (375°F.) for about 1½ hours (lower the heat while cooking, if necessary). To serve, lift the chicken onto a hot plate and pour the juices and vegetables over it. Buttery jacket-potatoes make a good accompaniment—they may be baked on a separate shelf in the oven at the same time. Pass round a green salad.

JUNIPER SAUERKRAUT

One 15¼-oz. tin, or 1 pint,
  sauerkraut
½ pint stock
1 onion, chopped
1 clove of garlic, chopped
1 apple, chopped

2 oz. butter or margarine
1 cup yoghurt, sour cream,
  or thick cream
5 to 8 juniper berries,
  crushed
1 teaspoon celery seed

Soften the onion, garlic, and apple in the butter over a low heat, add the crushed juniper berries and the sauerkraut, celery seed, and stock. Simmer for a few minutes. Cover and put in a slow oven (300°F.) for 45 to 60 minutes. At the last stir in the yoghurt or cream. Serve hot with grilled pork, veal, or sausages.

VEAL GRUYÈRE

2 lb. veal fillets
2 large onions, chopped
2 cloves of garlic, chopped
4 oz. butter
12 juniper berries, crushed

One 8-oz. packet of sliced
  Gruyère cheese
Soft breadcrumbs
Salt and pepper

Gently fry the onion and garlic in the butter until soft. Add the crushed juniper berries and a little salt and pepper. Transfer to a baking dish, lay the veal fillets on top of the onion, then add the slices of Gruyère cheese. Sprinkle thickly with breadcrumbs and bake in a moderate oven (350°F.) for 45 minutes.

MUSTARD SEED

Mustard is an annual herb, native to Europe, Asia, and North Africa. It is interesting to note that there are no poisonous plants in the order Cruciferae (so called because the flower petals resemble a Greek cross). Mustard is only one of many well-known plants belonging to this family: among them are such familiar flowers, herbs, and vegetables as sweet alyssum, candytuft, wallflowers, woad, cress, horseradish, and cauliflower.

Tender young leaves of mustard and cress are old favourites together as salad and garnishing herbs. Mustard greens make an excellent salad on their own: as the larger leaves are quite hot they make an interesting contrast to certain foods. The leaves are an aid to health as well, and are still thought by many people to be a help in clearing the blood.

Mustard poultices and foot-baths, also still highly thought of, are ancient remedies for colds, fevers, and sciatica.

The mustard plant reaches 3 to $3\frac{1}{2}$ feet in height and produces bright yellow flowers, followed by seed which may be dark red or, in the species *alba*, light yellow. In commerce both are blended together, sometimes with turmeric, to make powdered mustard. Another commercial form is a paste consisting of mustard powder, vinegar, sugar, and herbs; the ingredients added to the powder vary with each manufacturer. Whole mustard seed is extremely palatable, and may be used when the powder or paste will not do. One expects the seeds to be too hot to eat, but they are pleasantly nutty to bite on, the released flavour having only a mild tang of mustard.

Use mustard seed with discretion to begin with, increasing the amount as you become used to it. It goes into white sauce, mayonnaise, potato salad, cole slaw, steamed cabbage, herb butter (page 81), cheese dishes, and savoury spreads; it is used in fish, chicken, pork, and veal dishes, and is recommended for sprinkling over any salted meat while boiling; it is also a valuable addition to pickles and chutney. Lemon and Mustard Seed Chutney, the recipe given below, is one of the most refreshing of preserves to eat with cold meat and curries, and to pass round at barbecues, the only drawback being that because of its popularity the whole batch disappears too quickly!

HAM AND SWEET POTATO PIE

1½ lb. ham
1 lb. sweet potatoes
1 large onion
½ pint or 10-oz. tin onion
   soup

2 teaspoons mustard seed
2 tablespoons raw or brown
   sugar
A little butter
Salt and pepper

Slice the ham, cut it into pieces, and put it into an oven-proof dish. Peel the sweet potatoes and the onion, slice thinly, and put in layers over the ham, sprinkling each layer with mustard seed, salt, and pepper. Pour in the onion soup. Sprinkle the top with brown sugar, dot with butter, cover, and bake in a moderate oven (350°F.) for about 1 hour.

The ham may be replaced with cold corned beef, or with cold cooked salted mutton.

Place ¼ lb. butter in the oven in a baking dish, and when it is melted and sizzling, put in the fillets (dipped in milk and coated with fine breadcrumbs), and sprinkle them with salt, pepper, and 2 teaspoons mustard seed. Bake for 40 to 60 minutes in a moderate oven (350°F.), basting occasionally. If becoming dry, add more butter. Serve hot, pouring any excess butter over the fish. A large translucent grape, peeled, pipped, and resting on each fish, is an attractive garnish.

LEMON AND MUSTARD SEED CHUTNEY

4 *medium-sized onions*	1 *teaspoon ground allspice*
5 *big lemons*	1 *oz. mustard seed*
1 *oz. common salt*	1 *lb. sugar*
1 *pint cider vinegar*	¼ *lb. seedless raisins*

Peel and slice the onions, cut up the lemons (discard pips), sprinkle with the salt, and leave for 12 hours. Add the remaining ingredients, bring to the boil, and simmer until tender (about 45 minutes). Spoon into jars and seal when cool.

POPPY SEED

The slate-blue poppy-seed used for cooking is produced from an annual poppy that is native to Asia and came centuries ago to Europe, where it grows wild in great abundance. These attractive plants are often seen in herbaceous borders with other old-fashioned herbs and flowers, and most of us are familiar with the many colourful varieties, both annual and perennial, which have been evolved for decorative garden displays.

Poppy seed is free of narcotic content, and so is the valuable oil extracted from the seed: opium is obtained from the unripe heads of the poppy, *Papaver somniferum*. Morphine is a valuable product of opium. Of poppy's other medicinal virtues, Florence Ranson in *British Herbs* says: "Poppy-heads have long been a rural remedy for toothache, neuralgia and other nervous pains, and once it was common to see bunches of the dried heads hanging in chemists' shops." An infusion known as "the soporific sponge", made from poppy, mandrake, hemlock, and ivy, and poured over a sponge to be held under the nostrils, was highly regarded in the Middle Ages as an anaesthetic.

Poppy seed is used extensively in European and in Eastern cooking. The tiny grains are a natural source of minerals, and are so pleasant to use in food that a jarful in the kitchen is almost indispensable. The seed may be used whole or ground. When ground it is combined with eggs, mixed candied fruit, sugar, and spice to make a nourishing fat-free and flour-free cake; a rich filling of ground poppy-seed and other ingredients is made for strudels and ring cakes.

Whole poppy-seed has a vast number of uses; it is sprinkled on breads, rolls, cakes, pies, mashed potato, and whipped cream; it is excellent in white sauce for vegetables, and in honey dressing for fruit; it is mixed with cooked noodles and butter, or with macaroni.

CONTINENTAL POPPY-SEED CAKE

1½ cups poppy seed
6 eggs, separated
1 cup sugar

½ cup mixed candied
fruit-peel
1 teaspoon allspice

Grind the poppy seed in a grinder or electric blender, or have it ground at a Continental delicatessen. The seeds may sometimes be bought already ground. Beat the egg yolks until thick, and while still beating gradually add the sugar. Stir in the mixed peel, allspice, and ground poppy-seed. Beat the egg whites until stiff but not dry, and fold carefully and thoroughly into the poppy-seed mixture. Have ready a buttered and lightly floured spring-form cake tin, and pour in the cake mixture. Put it into a preheated slow to moderate oven (325°F.) and bake for about 50 minutes. Allow the cake to cool in the tin, then carefully remove the spring form. Spread the top of the cake with whipped cream before serving.

ALEXANDRA'S FRUIT AND POPPY-SEED PUDDING, COUNTRY STYLE

1½ cups self-raising flour
½ cup sugar
A lump of butter
Milk

1 tablespoon poppy seed
1 cup mixed candied
fruit-peel

A good neighbour, Alexandra, once baked and gave me this pudding when we were very busy. It was popular with every member of the family.

Rub the butter into the flour and sugar, and add enough milk to allow the mixture to be spread into a buttered oven-proof dish. Cover with the fruit peel and poppy seed, press-

ing well down, then sprinkle with a little sugar. Bake in a
moderate oven (375°F.). Eat hot or cold with cream.

POPPY-SEED NOODLES

To accompany grills, casseroles, rissoles, sauerbratten,
goulash, stews, or meat loaf.

Put a quantity of water into a large saucepan with a pinch
of salt and bring to the boil. Empty a packet of noodles into
the saucepan. Continue boiling for about 15 minutes, or until
the noodles are soft, stirring occasionally to prevent them
sticking together. Drain in a colander, running cold water
over them. Shake the noodles well and stand them on one
side. Rinse and dry the saucepan, put 1 dessertspoon butter
in and return it to the stove. Add the well-drained noodles
and 1 tablespoon poppy seed. Re-heat, mixing well together.
Serve immediately.

SESAME SEED

Sesame is an annual herb that is grown as an important food crop in many parts of the world today. It grows 3 to 4 feet high and bears white flowers that are followed by oil-bearing seeds high in protein and mineral content. The mature pods pop at the merest touch, scattering the small white seeds, and this makes harvesting with machinery difficult, though strains are now being grown that do not have this tendency.

Sesame is one of the earliest and most valuable herbs known to man. The name itself is associated with well-known fables, bringing to mind Ali Baba's magic words "Open, Sesame!" and the revealing of that glowing, jewel-filled cave.

Dorothy Bovée Jones says in *The Herbarist*: "There is some disagreement among authorities as to the exact center of origin for this ancient herb. It may have been Afghanistan, or Africa, or the Sunda Islands in the East Indies. It does not exist in a wild state today. It is mentioned in Sanskrit literature and in Egyptian scripts as well as in old Hebrew writings. Marco Polo wrote that he had had sesame oil in travelling through Persia, and thought it had a better flavour than any oil he had ever tasted." Cleopatra, wise in the art of cosmetics, is supposed to have used sesame oil as a skin beautifier.

A product of sesame seed is an edible opaque cream known as tahina, which has the consistency of honey and in taste resembles peanut butter. It is extremely popular in Arabic, Egyptian, Lebanese, and Greek food, and may be found in some Continental provision stores. Tahina mixed with cooked brown beans makes a Lebanese dish. Another favourite dish is made with cooked eggplant and tahina mashed to a paste: it is eaten cold as an hors-d'œuvre with pieces of bread. Tahina is sometimes thinned with a little lemon juice to make a nutty sauce for fish and shellfish; it is also palatable and nourishing when spread straight from the container onto bread and butter.

Tahina is an ingredient in the confection named Halvah, said to be Egyptian in origin and particularly popular with Greek, Syrian, and Jewish people—and with anyone else once they have tasted it. When chilled and cut into small blocks it makes an agreeable accompaniment to black coffee.

Sesame meal, which is ground sesame seed, is obtained from health-food shops; because it is so high in protein, vegetarians use quantities of it in their daily diet. The meal is used in various ways: it is sprinkled on salads and vegetables, and together with eggs and desiccated coconut it makes sustaining and pleasant-tasting little cakes.

Sesame seed and honey bars are delectable candies to be found in Continental delicatessens and cake shops. In fact, the flavour of sesame has a powerful attraction, and anything made with the seed, or any product from it, is delicious.

There are many quick and simple ways in which sesame seed may be introduced into everyday food:

Gently fry a tablespoon of sesame seed in butter until light brown, and either toss through a green salad or add to whipped potato, cream cheese, or mashed savoury avocado.

Toast the seed lightly and sprinkle it on cooked chicken and fish, cream soups, and fruit salads.

Sprinkle sesame seed on uncooked foods like scones, biscuits, cookies, rolls, or casseroles: the seed will brown during cooking.

Use sesame seed wherever you would use nuts in cooking, for a change.

SESAME AND OATMEAL COOKIES

2 *cups rolled oats*	1 *teaspoon salt*
¼ *cup sesame seed*	¾ *cup desiccated coconut*
¾ *cup raw sugar*	¼ *lb. butter, melted*

These are popular with children. To make, mix all the dry ingredients together, add the melted butter and stir it into the mixture. Press out onto a greased and floured tray. Bake in a moderate oven (375° to 400°F.) for 30 minutes. Cut into fingers when cold.

SESAME-SEED SALAD

1 *head of lettuce*	2 *tablespoons sesame seed*
½ *cup stoned black olives*	*Butter*
2 *tomatoes, quartered*	*French dressing (page 88)*

Wash and dry the lettuce, tear the leaves and put them into a salad bowl. Add the olives and tomatoes. Gently fry the sesame seed in butter until it is golden, add to the salad, and toss well with French dressing.

EGGPLANT AND TAHINA APPETIZER

This is delicious when served with thin slices of rye bread.

Peel and cut up an eggplant. Fry gently in butter until soft—about 10 minutes. Turn into a bowl and mash to a pulp or put into a blender. Add 1 teaspoon salt, 1 tablespoon lemon juice, 2 pulverized cloves of garlic, ¼ cup tahina, and 1 dessertspoon chopped mint. Blend all together.

Put the mixture into a dish and chill in the refrigerator, where it will set firm.

VANILLA BEANS

The vanilla bean comes from a perennial climbing orchid, a native of Central America. The golden flowers are followed by flat pods 6 inches in length, which when dried for culinary use are black and shiny like licorice. The perfume is sweet and permeating, and no substitute is considered suitable by connoisseurs, especially in the making of such dishes as French Ice Cream.

A piece of vanilla bean about 2 inches long should be cut, slit down the centre and used in ice creams, custards, and milk puddings, and infused in the milk for cake mixtures. The piece of bean may be rinsed and used several times. A good place for storing it is in a sugar canister, where the bean scents the sugar and remains dry and clean. Some people like to keep the vanilla bean in a little cognac, but to my way of thinking the true vanilla flavour is then overpowered. A recipe for Vanilla Sugar is given in this chapter.

FRENCH ICE CREAM

½ pint milk
½ pint heavy cream
2 inches of vanilla bean

6 eggs, separated
½ cup sugar

This is a smooth, rich ice cream for special occasions. Split the vanilla bean, put it into a saucepan with the milk, scald on a low flame, then stand the pan on one side. Whisk the egg yolks with the sugar, add to the milk, and stir over low heat until thick. Remove from the stove while still stirring. (If it curdles, beat with a rotary beater.) Whip the cream lightly and fold it into the custard. Pour into a chilled refrigerator tray and place in the freezing compartment. Stir once or twice during freezing.

FRENCH ICE CREAM AUX ABRICOTS

Make French Ice Cream as in the preceding recipe. Have ready 2 oz. diced glacé apricots which have been soaked in ¼ cup brandy or cognac for at least 2 hours or overnight. Fold into the ice cream before freezing it. A little apricot brandy may be poured over each serving as a sauce.

RICH VANILLA CUSTARD

¾ *pint milk*	*2 inches of vanilla bean*
Yolks of 2 eggs, and	*2 scant tablespoons sugar*
1 whole egg	*1 dessertspoon butter*

Split the vanilla bean and put it into a saucepan with the milk. Scald the milk, then stand the pan on one side. Beat the eggs with sugar, pour a little of the milk onto them, and return this to the saucepan. Add the butter, and stir over a low flame until thick. Take the pan off the stove and whip the contents with a rotary beater. Pour into a jug and allow to become cool.

VANILLA SUGAR

If you have an electric blender it is only a matter of seconds to make this scented sugar for sprinkling on top of custard, whipped cream, and stewed fruit, or to dust on biscuits before baking them.

Put 1 cup sugar into a blender, and break half a vanilla bean into pieces and add to the sugar. Blend on high speed until the bean is reduced to black flecks. Keep in a screw-top jar.

SOME BOOKS CONSULTED

The Herbarist. A publication of the Herb Society of America. Boston, Massachusetts, 1959.

Harmsworth's Universal Encyclopedia, Educational Book Co. Ltd., London.

Island Recipe Book, compiled by M. O. Blackwell and A. M. Blandy. Vila, New Hebrides, October 1947.

Leyel, Mrs C. F., *The Truth About Herbs*. Culpeper Press, 1954.

Lotions and Potions. A little book compiled by the National Federation of Women's Institutes, England, 1956. Printed by Novello & Co. Ltd.

Mrs Beeton's Book of Household Management. Ward Lock & Co. Ltd., London, 1906.

Ranson, Florence, *British Herbs*. Penguin Books, 1941, 1954.

Rohde, Eleanour Sinclair, *Herbs and Herb Gardening*. Medici Society, London, 1936.

Rohde, Eleanour Sinclair, *A Garden of Herbs*. Philip Lee Warner, Publisher to the Medici Society Ltd, London. Boston, U.S.A.

Thompson, Flora, *Lark Rise to Candleford*. Reprint Society, London, 1948.

Webster, Helen Noyes, *Herbs: How to Grow Them and How to Use Them*. Charles T. Branford Company, Boston, revised and enlarged edition 1947.

White, Florence, *Good English Food (Local and Regional)*. Jonathan Cape, London, 1952.

INDEX

A

Ale, mulled, 175
Alexandra's fruit and poppy-seed
  pudding, country style, 200
Allspice (Jamaica pepper), 1, 131-3
Anchusa, 13
Angelica, 11, 13, 18, 20-1
  candied, 20
  leaves and stewed rhubarb, 21
  tea, 119, 120
Anise cookies, 174
Aniseed, 3, 173-5
  carrots, 175
Appetizer, eggplant and tahina, 204
Apple,
  baked, 142
  crumble, coriander, 184
  jelly, 102
  pie, 1
  pudding, 144
  with geranium leaves, baked, 105
Applemint, 68
Apple-scented geraniums, 101
Arabian stuffed capsicums, 184
Aromatic bath, 61, 126
Aromatic seeds, 173-206
Aromatic sweet potatoes, 182
Artemisia (family of herbs), 107
Aspic,
  basil and tomato, 28
  cabbage, 182
Attar-of-roses sponge, 104
Avocado,
  and chervil, iced, 42
  mould, crab and, 108
  soup, 156

B

Bags,
  lavender, 124
  sweet, 124, 125
Baked apples with geranium leaves, 105
Baked fish with cider, 100
Baked pears and cardamom, 180
Baked tomatoes and basil, 27
Baked veal chops, 48
Baked beans, barbecued, 136
Balm, 2, 17, 22-4
  and marshmallow custard, 23
  and orange frosted, 23
  dressing for orange salad, 23
  lemon, 13, 22-4
  tea, 119
  variegated, 13, 22
Balsam, 7, 8
Bananas, flaming, 140
Barbecued baked beans, 136
Basil, 2, 4, 9, 13, 25-9
  and tomato aspic, 28
  baked tomatoes and, 27
  bush, 25
  lamb's fry with, 27
  sweet, 13, 16, 17, 25

Bath,
  aromatic, 61
  aromatics for the, 126
  cosmetic, 38
Bay leaf, 3, 30-2
  and pickled walnuts, steak casserole
    with, 32
Beans, sweet-sour brown, 140
Bechamel sauce, 116
Beef,
  and tomatoes, 86
  teriyaki, 152
Beetroot and cardamom salad, iced, 180
Bergamot (bee-balm), 8, 11, 13, 33-5
  orange, 34
  pork sausages with apple and, 34
  salad, 34
  sauce, 35
Berries, juniper, 193-5
Black pepper, 159-60
Borage, 8, 14, 17, 36-8
Bortsch, 144
Bouillabaisse, 163
Box, 11
Bread,
  dough, 76
  sage, 95
Buddleia, 8
Buns, saffron, 162
Burning steak, 66
Butter, parsley, 81
Buttered cabbage spines and rosemary, 85-6
Buttered marrow, 115
Buttered zucchini, 115

C

Cabbage,
  aspic, 182
  leaves, stuffed, 32
  spines and rosemary, buttered, 85
Cake,
  continental poppy-seed, 200
  coriander honey, 184-5
  rich spiced christmas, 141
  seed sponge, 178
  spiced tea, 49
Cambridge Scarlet, 33
Candied angelica, 20
Candied rose petals, 90
Candles, scented, 127
Capsicums, Arabian stuffed, 184
Caraway, 176-8
  rice ring and tuna, 177
  thyme, 113
Cardamom, 179-80
  baked pears and, 180
  honey dressing, 180
  salad, iced beetroot and, 180
Carnation, 37
Carrots, aniseed, 175
Casserole,
  sausages in cider, 57
  with bay leaves and pickled walnuts,
    steak, 32

with pork sausages, red cabbage, 174
Cayenne pepper, 134-5
Celery seed, 181-2
Chamomile, 13, 15, 118, 119, 120
  tea, 120
Cheese,
  dip or spread, dill-, 189
  dressing, mint and, 71
  in the shell, pineapple and, 177
  omelet, Isabelle's sage and, 95
  straws, 135
Chervil, 11, 13, 17, 39-42
  iced avocado and, 42
Chicken,
  curry, hot, 149
  juniper, 193
  livers in wine, 109
  mimosa, 110
  mould, 116
  stuffing for, 116
  supreme with peaches, 108
Chicory, 13, 18, 43-4
  and eggs, 43
  salad, 44
Chili, 3, 136-7
  con carne, 3, 137
Chives, 9, 11, 13, 17, 18, 45-7
  French omelet with, 46
Chutney, lemon and mustard seed, 197
Cinnamon, 1, 138-41
Clorinda (geranium), 103
Clove orange *see* pomander ball
Clove-pinks, 14
Cloves, 142-5
Coathanger, scented, 125
Cocktail, pineapple, 72
Coconut-scented geranium, 103
Cole-slaw with dill, 52
Continental poppy-seed cake, 200
Cooked fennel, 54
Cookies,
  anise, 174
  sesame and oatmeal, 204
Coriander, 13, 48-9, 183-5
  apple crumble, 184
  honey cakes, 184
  marmalade flavoured with, 49
Cosmetic bath, 38
Cottage pie, 64
Crab,
  and avocado mould, 108
  paprika, ten-minute, 158
Creamed cucumber, 46
Cress, 10
Crystallized flowers, 37
Crystallized mint leaves, 72
Cucumber,
  creamed, 46
  Turkish, 186
Cumin, 186-7
  and rose geranium drops, 187
Curry,
  hot chicken, 149
  Indian, 147
  Indonesian, 148
  meat, 148
  powder, 146-9

Custard,
  balm and marshmallow, 23
  caramel, 37
  mint and marshmallow, 71
  rich vanilla, 206

D

Devonshire junket, 140
Dill, 3, 13, 50-2, 188-9
  -cheese dip or spread, 189
  cole-slaw with, 52
  pickles, 50
  sauce, 189
  scallops with, 51
Dip or spread, dill-cheese, 189
Dolmas, 27
Dressing,
  cardamom honey, 180
  French, 27, 167
  mint and cheese, 71
  dumplings, tomato, 135
  sunny saffron, 163

E

Egg,
  and potato pie, 135
  chicory and, 43
  sandwiches with caraway thyme, 113
  tart, minted, 71
Eggplant and tahina appetizer, 204
Emily's pastry, 94

F

Fair Ellen (geranium), 103
Fennel, 2, 13, 50, 53-5
  cooked, 54
  cream sauce, 54
  Florence, 17, 53, 54, 190
  sweet, 53
  tea, 192
Fennel seed, 190-2
  potato cake, 192
  sausage, 54
Festive ham, 143
Fillets of fish meuniere, 197
Fish meuniere,
  fillets of, 197
  pie with herbs, 47
  roe entree, 29
  savory stuffing for, 99
  special, 31
  supreme, 155
  with cider, baked, 100
Flaming bananas, 140
Foxglove, 14
French dressing, 27, 167
French ice cream, 205
French ice cream aux abricots, 206
French lavender, 11, 12, 14, 60
French omelet with chives, 46
French-style peas, 70
Fried orange slices, 132
Fried parsley, 82
Fried tripe and winter savory, 99
Fruit and poppy-seed pudding country
  style, Alexandra's, 200

G

Garden thyme, 112
Garlic, 56-8
Geraniums, scented-leaved, 14, 17,
  101-105
  apple-scented, 101
  clorinda *variety*, 103
  coconut-scented, 103
  Fair Ellen *variety*, 103
  jelly, rose, 132
  nutmeg-scented, 101
  peppermint-scented, 102
  Robert, 103
  rose-scented, 101
  southernwood *variety*, 103
Gift packages, 126
Ginger, 150-3
Glazed pears, 21
Gooseberry shortcake, saffron, 164
Goulash, Hungarian veal, 158
Green salad with rose petals, 89

H

Hair rinse, rosemary, 87
Hair tonic, 96
Halvah, 203
Ham,
  and sweet potato pie, 198
  festive, 143
Haricot beans with tomatoes, 40
Heliotrope, 14
Hemlock, 2
Henbane, 2
Herbal teas, 118-121
Herbs, 1-127
  bouquet of, 30
  drying of, 15-16
  garden, 7-14, 16
  growing in containers, 17-19
  lawn, 15
  medicinal, 2, 118-121
  sandwiches, 9-10
  scones, 65
Hollandaise sauce, 106, 109
Hollyhocks, 14
Honey,
  cakes, coriander, 184
  of roses, 90
  soap, 127
Honeysuckle, 14
Hot chicken curry, 149
Hot slaw, 189
Hungarian goulash, 3
Hungarian veal goulash, 158
Hyssop, 11, 13

I

Ice cream,
  aux abricots, French, 206
  French, 205
Iced avocado and chervil, 42
Iced beetroot and cardamom salad, 180
Indian curry, 147

Indonesian curry, 148
Isabelle's sage and cheese omelet, 95
Italian parsley, 79

J

Jamaica pepper *see* allspice
Jam, rose-petal, 89
Jasmine, 14
Jelly,
  mint, 72
  parsley, 81-2
  peppermint, 104
  rose geranium, 132
  savory and grape-juice, 98
Juniper,
  berries, 193-5
  chicken, 193-4
  sauerkraut, 194
Junket, Devonshire, 140

K

Kedgeree, 168
Kidneys and mushrooms, 191

L

Labiatae, 4
Lad's love, 11, 107
Lady Plymouth (geranium), 101
Lamb's fry with basil, 27
Lamb,
  haricot, 81
  savory stuffed leg of, 98
  shanks Armenian, 187
Lavender, 11, 13, 14, 17, 59-62
  bags, 124
  English, 12, 14, 60, 61
  sugar, 61
  vinegar, 62
  water without distillation, 61
Lavender-cotton, 12
Leek tart with sage, 93
Lemon and mustard seed chutney, 197
Lemon-scented baked custard, 104
Lemon-scented geranium (verbena), 14, 102
Lemon thyme, 112
  tea, 119
Lentils, sausages and, 160
Lovage, 13, 18

M

Mace, 154
Mandragora (mandrake), 2
Mandrake *see* mandragora
Mango mousse, 151
Majoram, 9, 13, 15, 16, 17, 18, 63-7
  sweet, 63
  vinegar, 67
Marmalade flavoured with coriander, 49
Marrow, buttered, 115
Mayonnaise, sharp, 182
Meat,
  balls, savory, 115
  curry, 148
  loaf, savory, 117

Mexican guacamole, 137
Milk, rabbit cooked in, 117
Mint, 4, 13, 14, 17, 18, 37, 68-73
   and cheese dressing, 71
   and marshmallow custard, 71
   bergamot, 68
   curly, 69
   eau-de-cologne, 10, 68
   jelly, 72
   julep, 72
   leaves, crystallized, 72
   menthol, 68
   sauce, 70
   teas, 119, 121
   tea, sparkling, 121
Minted egg tart, 71
Mitcham peppermint, 68
Monosodium glutamate, 160
Mother of thyme, 113, 114
Mould,
   chicken, 116
   crab and avocado, 108
Mousse, mango, 151
Mulled ale, 175
Mushrooms,
   kidneys and, 191
   noodles and, 81
Mustard, 10
Mustard seed, 196-8
   chutney, lemon and, 197

N

Nettle tea, 119, 121
Newburg sauce, 134
Noodles,
   and mushrooms, 81
   poppy-seed, 201
Note-paper, scented, 127
Nutmeg, 154-6
Nutmeg-scented geranium, 101

O

Old woman, 107
Olives oregano, 78
Omelet,
   Isabelle's sage and cheese, 95
   with chives, French, 46
Onions, pickled, 160
Orange slices, fried, 132
Oregano, 4, 13, 15, 17, 74-9
   olives, 78
Orris root, 122
Oswego tea, 35
Oysters bercy, 66

P

Packages, gift, 126
Papaw pickle, 149
Paprika, 3, 157-8
Parsley, 9, 10, 11, 13, 17, 18, 30, 79-82
   butter, 81
   curled, 79
   fern leaves, 79
   fried, 82
   ice, 82

   Italian, 79
   jelly, 81
Pastry, Emily's, 94
Peaches, chicken supreme with, 108
Pears,
   and cardamom, baked, 180
   glazed, 21
Peas, French-style, 70
Pennyroyal, 7, 9, 11, 13, 15, 17, 69
Pepper,
   black and white, 159-60
   cayenne, 134-5
Peppermint, 68-9
   jelly, 104
   tea, 119, 120
Peppermint-scented geranium, 102
Pickled onions, 160
Pickle, papaw, 149
Pie,
   apple, 1-2
   cottage, 64
   egg and potato, 135
   ham and sweet potato, 198
   pizza, 75
   potato, 67
   shepherd's, 64
Pimento see allspice
Pineapple,
   and cheese in the shell, 177
   clove-spiced hot, 143
   cocktail, 72
Pizza pie, 75
Pomander ball, (clove orange), 122, 123, 142
Poppy seed, 199-201
   cake, continental, 200
   noodles, 201
   pudding country style, Alexandra's
   fruit and, 200
Pork, boiled salt, 142
   sausages, red cabbage casserole with, 174
   with apple and bergamot, 34
Potato,
   cake fennel seed, 192
   pie, 67
   pie, egg and, 135
   salad, tropical, 168
   soup, 41
Pot-pourri, 60, 90-1, 103, 122, 131
Poultry stuffing, 116
Primroses, 14
Pudding,
   apple, 144
   rice and treacle, 31

Q

Quiche lorraine, 78

R

Rabbit cooked in milk, 117
Red cabbage casserole with pork
   sausages, 174
Red tomato relish, 152
Relish, red tomato, 152
Rhubarb and angelica leaves, stewed, 21
Rice,
   and treacle pudding, 31

ring and tuna, caraway, 177
Rich spiced Christmas cake, 141
Rich vanilla custard, 206
Risotto, saffron, 162
Robert (geranium), 103
Rose, 14, 37, 88-91
   creams, 132
   honey of, 90
   water, 91
Rose geranium,
   drops, cumin and, 187
   jelly, 132
Rosemary, 4, 11, 12, 13, 14, 17, 83-7
   buttered cabbage spines and, 85
   hair rinse, 87
   rubbing lotion, 126
   scones, 86
   snow, 87
   tea, 119, 121
Rose petals,
   candied, 90
   green salad with, 89
   jam, 89
Rose-scented geranium, 101
Rubbing lotion, rosemary, 126
Rue, 13, 14

S

Saffron, 1, 3, 4, 161-4
   buns, 162
   dumplings, 163
   gooseberry shortcake, 164
   risotto, 162
Sage, 11, 13, 17, 92-6
   and cheese omelet, Isabelle's, 95
   and onion stuffing, 94
   bread, 95
   cheese spread, 92
   hair tonic, 96
   leek tart with, 93
   tea, 96
   Welsh rarebit with, 94
Salad,
   balm dressing for orange, 24
   bergamot, 34
   chicory, 44
   iced beetroot and cardamom, 180
   seafood, 41
   sesame-seed, 204
   tropical potato, 168
   waldorf, 157
   with rose petals, green, 89
Salt, 165-6
   seasoned, 166
Salt pork, boiled, 142
Sauces,
   bearnaise, 106, 109
   bechamel, 116
   bergamot, 35
   dill, 189
   fennel cream, 54
   French dressing, 107
   hollandaise, 106, 109
   mayonnaise, 106
   mint, 70
   newburg, 134

   sage, 96
   savory tomato, 98
   sour cream, 106
   supreme, 110
   tartare, 106, 108
Sauerkraut, juniper, 194
Sausages,
   and lentils, 160
   fennel-seed, 54
   in cider, casserole, 57
   red cabbage casserole with pork, 174
   with apple and bergamot, pork, 34
Savory, 97-100
   and grape-juice jelly, 98
   fried tripe and winter, 99
   meat balls, 115
   meat loaf, 117
   stuffed leg of lamb, 98
   stuffing for fish, 99
   tomato sauce, 98
   winter, 11, 13, 17
Savory Welsh rarebit, 156
Scallops with dill, 51
Scented candles, 127
Scented coathanger, 125
Scented note-paper, 127
Scented-leaved geraniums, 101-5
Scones,
   herb, 65
   rosemary, 86
Seafood salad, 41
Seeds, aromatic, 173-206
Seed sponge cake, 178
Sesame seed, 202-4
   and oatmeal cookies, 204
   salad, 204
Sharp mayonnaise, 182
Shepherd's thyme, 114
Shortcake, saffron gooseberry, 164
Soap, honey, 127
Soup,
   avocado, 156
   potato, 41
   spinach, 41
Southernwood,
   (artemisia), 107
   (geranium), 103
Spaghetti bolognese, 3, 77
Sparkling mint tea, 121
Spearmint, 10, 68
Spiced tea cake, 49
Spiced veal roll, 131
Spiced vinegar, 160
Spices, 127-169
Spinach soup, 41
Sponge cake, seed, 178
Spread,
   dill-cheese dip or, 189
   sage-cheese, 92
Steak,
   burning, 66
   casserole with bay leaves and
   pickled walnuts, 32
   kebabs, 75
   rolls, stuffed, 57
Stewed rhubarb and angelica leaves, 21

Stew, Welsh, 31
Sticadove, 60
Stuffed cabbage leaves, 32
Stuffed steak rolls, 57
Stuffing, for fish, savory, 99
    for poultry (thyme), 115
    for sage and onion, 94
    for turkey, 116
Summer vegetable tart, 65
Sunny saffron dumplings, 163
Sweet bags, 124, 125
Sweet potato pie, ham and, 198
Sweet potatoes, aromatic, 182
Sweet-sour brown beans, 140

T

Tahina, 202
    appetizer, eggplant and, 204
Tarragon, 4, 14, 17, 106-10
    spicy, 13
    vinegar, 107, 110
Tartare sauce, 106, 108
Tart,
    leek with sage, 93
    minted egg, 71
    summer vegetable, 65
    treacle, 139
Tea,
    angelica, 119, 120
    balm, 119
    chamomile, 120
    fennel, 192
    lemon-thyme, 119
    mint, 119-121
    nettle, 119, 121
    oswego, 35
    peppermint, 119, 120
    rosemary, 119, 121
    sparkling mint, 121
Teas, herbal, 118-121
Ten-minute crab paprika, 158
Thyme, 2, 4, 9, 11, 12, 15, 17, 30,
    107-11
    caraway, 113
    fragrant, 13
    garden, 112
    lemon, 112
    mother of, 113, 114
    shepherd's, 114
    variegated, 113
    westmoreland, 114
Tisanes see herbal teas
Toddy, 138
Tomato,
    and basil aspic, 28

    and basil, baked, 27
    beef and, 86
    dumplings, 135
    haricot beans with, 40
    relish, red, 152
Treacle tart, 139
Tripe and winter savory, fried, 99
Tropical potato salad, 168
Tuna, caraway rice ring and, 177
Turkey stuffing, 115
Turkish cucumbers, 186
Turmeric, 167

V

Vanilla,
    beans, 205-6
    custard, rich, 206
    sugar, 206
Variegated thyme, 113
Vatroushki, 145
Veal,
    chops, baked, 48
    goulash, Hungarian, 158
    Gruyere, 194
    in apple juice, 66
    roll, spiced, 131
Vegetable tart, summer, 65
Vinegar,
    lavender, 62
    marjoram, 67
    rose, 89
    spiced, 160
    tarragon, 107, 110
Violets, 14, 37

W

Waldorf salad, 157
Wallflower, 12, 14
Welsh rarebit,
    savory, 156
    with sage, 94
Welsh stew, 31
Westmoreland thyme, 114
White pepper, 159-60
Wild thyme, 113
Wine, chicken livers in, 109
Winter savory, 11, 13, 17
    fried tripe and, 99
Wormwood, 11, 12, 107

Z

Zucchini, buttered, 115